SELLER!

THE LIFE & DEATH OF ERIC PODE OF CROYDON

by
Andrew Marshall & David Renwick

London
GEORGE ALLEN & UNWIN
Boston Sydney

First published in 1981

George Allen & Unwin (Publishers) Ltd
40 Museum Street, London WC1A 1LU

British Library Cataloguing in Publication Data

Marshall, Andrew
Bestseller: the life and death of Eric Pode of Croydon.
I. Title II. Renwick, David
827' .914 PR6063.A/

ISBN 0-04-827036-9

Design and illustration: Alan Kitching/Ron Sandford/Martin Lee
Photography of cover, end papers and authors by Michael Dyer Associates

Printed in Great Britain
by William Clowes Ltd, Beccles and London

CONTENTS

ACKNOWLEDGEMENTS

The Radio Times Picture Library for the picture of the *Radio Times* on page 29; The Palaeontology Department of the British Museum for permission to reproduce the joke by Benny Hill on page 133; The Pope, for permission to reproduce; Andy Jones, Chris Rhys-Chrys, Andy Evans-Davies, Al Wyatt-Trodd-Heskwith, Tenniel Quock-Alfalfa, Dorothy Spam-Kilby and Andy Atkins, Melvin Andys, Andy Chris-Stevenson-Andy, Chris Dudgeon-Gurnhill and the Adams Boys, Andy Evan-Andrews, Andy Andy Andy Andy Andy Andy Chris Rothschild-Atkins and Martin Anderry, Richard Chris-Toffson, and Howard Curtis-Andyson for permission to reproduce the two-line quickie from Not the Nine O'Clock News on page 13⅛.

All Eric Pode of Croydon's gowns in this book by SPIT of Luton; special thanks to Mr Herbert Diss of Catford for the unpleasant skin disease on page 37; not very special thanks to Mr Edith Dong, a part-time mummified thrush with London Weekend's Forward Planning Committee for the extract from Churning the Crap; the BBC for special dispensation to screw Esther Rantzen's armpits to a tactical-guided missile of the Pershing-2 class; Julie Andrews for releasing My Favourite Things when firemen had failed; Jilly Cooper for nothing.

Extra special gratitude for back-up whackerie on The Burkiss Way since 1976 to: Jo Kendall, Chris Emmett, Nigel Rees, Fred Harris, Denise Coffey, Simon Brett, John Lloyd, David Hatch, John Mason, Douglas Adams, Eric Young, John Whitehall, Martha Knight and Lisa Braun.

To the Radio Times Hulton Picture Library grateful thanks for much patient research and for assorted photographs of poets, politicians, spies, heroes and students.

HOW TO READ THIS BOOK

1 Lay the book on a dull, flat surface. Or any Nolan Sister. But preferably the book.

2 Take up a prostrate position, such as Head of British Rail.

3 Open the book. This can be done by inserting a crowbar between pages 21 and 22 and then dropping a small replica of Barry Manilow onto it from a great height. Alternatively you can use a large replica of Barry Manilow; or a large Barry Manilow of a replica. Better still, just drop Barry Manilow from a great height and forget the book.

4 Place the word you wish to read underneath an eye. This can be found dangling at the end of the optic nerve. If it feels large, grey and lumpy you may have got the wrong end.

5 Read two or three words every four hours as required, remembering not to exceed one and a half paragraphs in any 24 hours. Most of the jokes in this book are soluble in water, the sort doctors prefer; and almost all the ideas are specially whacky-shaped for easier swallowing.

6 If you bought this book from a reputable dealer it should have come to you in a special polythene bag.

WARNING: Having removed the polythene bag, place it over a child's head.

THIS BOOK CONTAINS:

1·102 million def. artic., nouns; 0·861 ml verbs; 0·0061ml adj.; 0·0053ml prep. cl.; 0·000367407503105741030410376296l873ml figures; 0·00012ml dram. iron.; 0·00007ml dead horses; 0·0000ml laughs.

EACH PAGE CONSTITUTES: 13·1% INSULTS
10·9% M'CAP.
6·3% PRINTER'S INK
69·7% WHITE PAPER

CONTAINS NO COLOURINGS

FOREWORD

By Professor
Sir Hugo Gradner, M.A.
Lecturer in English
and Contemporary Social
Studies at York University

In the broad sweep of contemporary English literature there are probably few figures whose richness of social vision engages our imagination quite so prolifically as those authors committed to a more critically naturalistic awareness of the worthless assurances buttressing our reactions against the environmental factors that shape and determine our everyday approach to life. Put less succinctly, we find them employing less of a double-pronged attack on the superficiality of existence through which it is possible to offer readily cogent if unstable solutions of a pragmatic order to common uncertainty, yet ignoring the embittered plea for a humane consciousness of the plight of morality, and more of a semblance of surface symbolism, delineating by its tension-evincing rhetoric the contrast in style evaluation between those whose aim it is to compel an appraisal of intrinsic cynicism through a less mechanically bogged-down exploration of problems and solutions, and those for whom the more subliminal awakening of a critique on our corrupting paradoxes is achieved in the less standard prosaic form of implicit nihilistic allusion.

This may seem a platitude. Yet when we come to analyse the advance of the so-called "popular radicals" in the field of post-Joycian absurdism, wading through the sterile morass of the Sallingerists and neo-Orwellian stoics, we find that all too often the competitive emotions of love and fear merge into a self-destructive anarchic passionism in a tableauesque branch of that dimension in modern-day literary syntax commonly referred to as "stunted inwardism"; further, that upon closer examination of the underlying linguistic alliance between Tzara-oriented vacuity and florid conformism we see, not the blueprint for synecdochic transference that one would have expected, but a reliance, justifiable in part, due to the clear interconnectedness of character-plot assimilation, upon the formulation of, in a sense, Bretonite abandonment of conventional metonymy and the use of the more familiar stock in trade, fabrical causality, i.e. lateral extension of the figurative discontinuity between that alignment which is part and parcel of the counter-reference-style "reticular matrix" approach by which we are now so overawed. And here, in a way, is the real crux of the problem. What is the basic *motivation*, in short the rational essence of logicality, in continually bombarding the reader with this albeit classically accepted literary standard: the piss-boring foreword?

Here indeed we have an enigma of truly macroistic proportionalism. Commissioned inevitably from some ranting study in chronic senility such as yours truly, they chart the depths of tedium like nobody's business. My God, they're *awful*. And you complain about them? You think *you're* getting a raw deal? Listen, all *you* have to do is flick through the things, completely ignoring pages I to XXXIV and getting straight on to the story you bought the book for in the first place. I have to *write* this bleeding rubbish. I have to sit up till the early hours looking up long words like synecdochic and metonymy! Three weeks these buggers take on average, constructing every sentence with a slide rule and ending up with something looking like an explosion in a Thesaurus factory! Well I've had enough of it! I've had your cruddy "allegorical labyrinth of figuratisms" up to here! So for mercy's sake leave this page NOW. Stop reading this garbage and give me a break. I said stop reading it!

Look, stop! Will you stop reading this page and move on to the next one! Are you mad? Why are you *still* reading this?

I don't believe this! Get on to the next page, you dyslexic cretin! Stop looking at these words! STOP IT, I SAID! STOP READING THIS PAGE!!!

A message from

NIGEL REES...

Hallo booklovers everywhere, and thankyou for welcoming me into your homes, to share the wonderful experience of this wild volume of whacky comedy which, I know, you will treasure for always, even when the jokes are 100 years old. A week next Tuesday. Well, it isn't one of *my* books, I'm afraid, but you can't have everything. Fortunately there *are* still plenty of *my* books – available right now from your local Allenandunwin dealer! There's the brand-new "Quote Unquote" book, the brand-new catchphrase book, and of course the ever popular "Things scrawled on walls", at only 95p in paperback – a mere 94p dearer than visiting t Gents at Waterloo and seeing it all for yours f. Ha ha, just my li joke there. No need to tak ffence, Grann ause there's also best-selling "Knitting Patt Rule 2K", featu g woolly witticisms have you in stitches! Ideal at difficult aunty at Christmas! Yes, it all there in my books – apho and apothegms, bon mots and bromides, gaffes and goofs, jollies a es, squibs and squelches, trobs and twaggles, vurklies and vo argtibots and wistos, z bdobbs and zoozlies, zurhhhhh ciess . . .*

* *We apologise for this breakdown in Nigel Rees. While fat felt-tip pens are being waved under his nose to revive his signature, please continue with the rest of the book . . .*

The name of Eric Pode of Croydon is not, perhaps, one that is very familiar to the average reader. During his not inconsiderable lifetime he made little if any real impact with his literary offerings. And indeed, aside from a few of his brief, welcome personal appearances on the humourous wireless programme The Burkiss Way (many of them still retained in BBC Archives we are assured), the legacy of his work was thought, until recently, to be very sparse indeed.

A few months ago, all that changed. A windfall, in the form of a hitherto unrecorded collection of papers and cuttings, suddenly came into our possession. The following extracts taken from the letter which accompanied them will make most of the facts of their discovery clear:

Anglia Television
Norwich Municipal Abattoir
Norwich NOR P1G.

5 May 1981

Dear Mr Marshall and Mr Renwick,

As you know, until the Year of Our Lord Grade 68, I was but a humble employee at ATV's Elstree Studios, where I worked on situation comedies, showing laughter buttons to their seats. Then, when I was old enough to die, I took the elixir of eternal senility, and was fortunate enough to secure a place here at Anglia's combined TV Network and Municipal Abattoir Operations in Norwich . . . where I now do talk loik this since this be a 'how all folk talks in the East of England, and has to have string toied round thy waist after this fashion what mine is now, see? Ar it be roight old fun here at . . . A couple of weeks ago I was attending a top-level meeting of the Programme Development and Goat Speying Committee, when I received a communication on that there talkie instrument with them new fangled wires coming out on it, how it do work I don't . . . from my wife to say that while cleaning out her grandfather she had come across an old strong-box what was a 'covered in dirt and cobwebs and such dust as you han't never sawed much the loikes of that hoighly interesting lump o'mud we ascreened at peak hour last . . . and found that the box was in fact securely fastened with ten padlocks which were impossible to open. Fortunately all the contents were on the outside, so it didn't matter. Continuity Gaffer ran his glass eye over they and he do say that the . . .ar, bet thy boots that . . . in his opinion that they may be authentic artefacts from the collection of a Mr Eric Pod of Crayfish (sp?). I am therefore sending them on to you as I feel you may better be able to assess their true worth since what you be a'educated gents the loikes of what Oi never had no proper . . .

Yours beyond treatment,
Royston Turnoff,
Controller of Programmes & Chief Pig Disemboweller,
ANGLIA TELEVISION LTD

The artefacts in question were soon shown to be of startling significance. That they were indeed once the original possessions of Croydon was quickly verified by a team of microbacteriologists and specialists in fungoid disorders. Not only do they include a whole host of stories, book fragments, screenplays and half-finished ideas of one sort or another, but what is of considerable interest is the additional collection of old diary entries, press cuttings, personal jottings and correspondence to and from publishers and television companies. In short, here was a treasure trove of writings and memorabilia which put the literary output of Eric Pode of Croydon in a thoroughly new light.

In this book we have attempted to present, in chronological order, a selection from these writings and documents. Diary extracts, letters and telegrams accompany the pieces of work in correct sequence, so that the reader may gain for herself a sense of Croydon's progression of style. What is probably most striking is the sheer *versatility* of Croydon's pen. From radio scripts to film treatments, from short essays to novels, from copy writing on TV commercials to ghost-writing autobiographies, there isn't one thing he has not failed miserably at. Our one overriding aim, therefore, has been to include as many *different* samples of his work as possible. Some editing has been inevitable, and we have included appropriate annotations and footnotes where further explanation was thought necessary.

In the general compilation of these manuscripts we are indebted to the Trustees of the Eric Pode of Croydon Estate and the shovel that was used to clear it up, as well as to The Crystals, for the biographical notes which follow.

Andrew Marshall & David Renwick
September, 1981

WHO WAS ERIC PODE OF CROYDON?

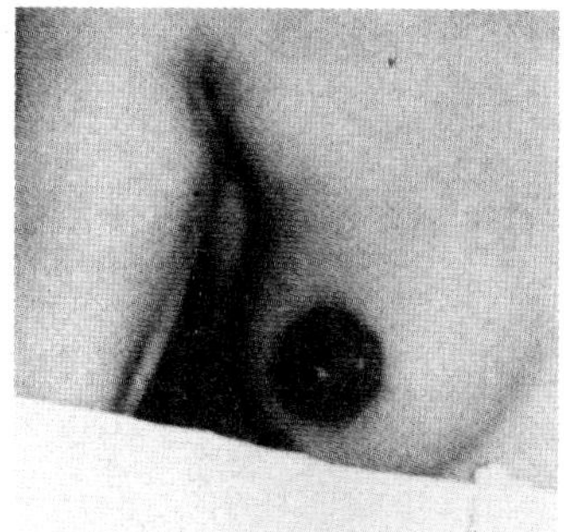

Samantha
. . . he got eighteen months

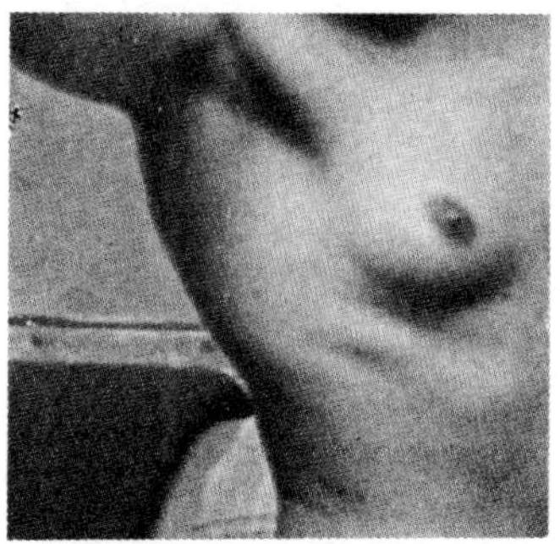

Julie
. . . two years' probation.

Sue
. . . nine months and the artichoke confiscated.

Eric Pode of Croydon was born Catford Edwin Sewage-works in 1926, nine months premature; his father going prematurely bald about the same time. In 1928, his mother, who had twenty-three other children and two eyelids to support, left their home in Barnsley and went to live. But it wasn't long before the spectre of poverty loomed large. On 13 August that year Croydon's father had to put the cat down after they were forced to sell the front-room carpet. Resolved that he really could afford no more children, Mr Croydon Sen. made an appointment to see a short-sighted conkers player, and thereafter got work doing voice-overs for Allan Ball. Da doo ron ron ron da doo ron ron.

At school, young Croydon proved he had an IQ equal to none. He was thrown out at the mental age of six to become a BBC sports commentator, and later went on to work for the *Radio Times*, cutting out little jagged patterns down the side of each page with a pair of nail scissors. It was around this time that he wrote his first short story. He was given six months suspended for two years and the judge ordered the lavatory wall to be destroyed. Despite this setback Croydon remained unbowed. He continued to write, and to hawk round his various submissions throughout life, undeterred by the inevitably brutal rejections his work inspired. Da doo ron ron ron da doo ron ron.

In 1941 Croydon was generally unhappy with his lot, and had part of it removed. Life seemed empty, but in the spring of that year he met a girl who changed everything, especially her socks. Her name was Dorothy and neither was his. And, during that summer he gradually became her closest friend, until eventually her father prized him off with a crowbar. The following April they married, fell in love, and moved into a little cottage on the outskirts of Robert Morley. The marriage, for some unaccountable reason, never worked, and four years later his wife got divorced in white. Da doo ron ron ron da doo ron ron.

Over the years a number of women fell passionately in love with Croydon, the number being nought. Altogether he had seventeen wives, and asked for six others to be taken into consideration. From 1976 to 1980, Croydon was offered walk-on parts in the humourous wireless programme The Burkiss Way. All seemed fine till he found out what he had to walk on. Yet, as the "spotty little lugworm's dropping" on Burkiss he received up to one fan letter a week, and frequently less. Complete strangers would now come up to him in the street and say "Eeurghhhh!!" And, ever after, Croydon always maintained that the happiest days of his working life were those spent recovering from food poisoning in the BBC canteen of a Friday evening at Burkiss recordings. Da doo ron ron ron da doo ron ron.

Sadly, the autographed photo of a boil which Croydon was paid for his weekly performance on The Burkiss Way was not enough to keep the wolves away from the door, and eventually he had to let them out. Things went from bad to worse, and from worse to a building society. In January 1980, Eric Pode of Croydon took the only way out. He was found by neighbours on the morning of the 17th, having put his head inside the door at Transport House. He had died at 11.30 the previous night. Six weeks later, he was dead. And four weeks after that, he was crowned Miss United Kingdom at the Empire Ballroom, Leicester Square. Da doo ron ron ron da doo ron ron.

(Taken from tracks 3, 5, 6 and 8,
"The Crystals' Greatest Hits",
Tamla-Motown, TM 1006 S.)

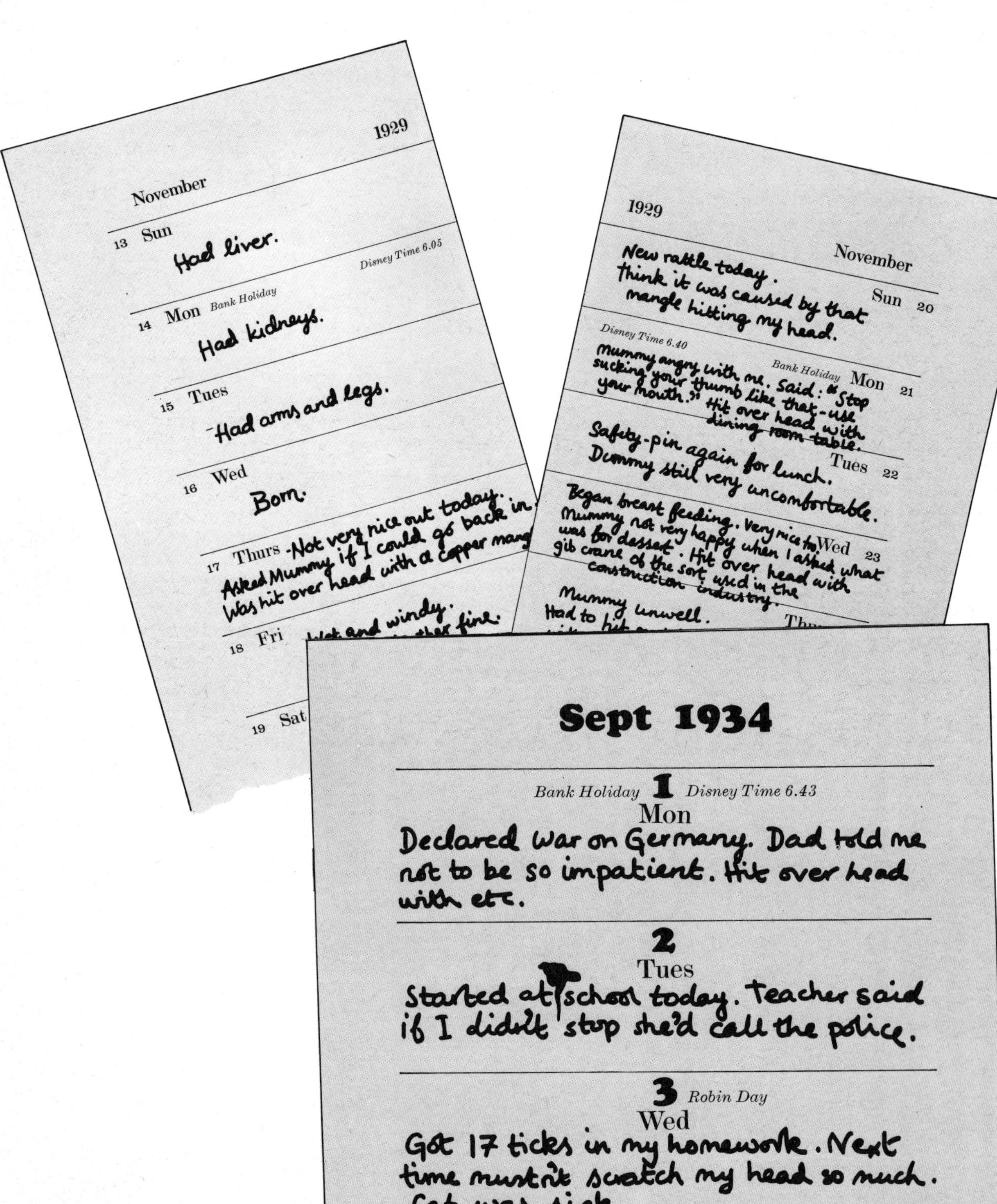

1929

November

13 Sun
Had liver.

Disney Time 6.05

14 Mon Bank Holiday
Had kidneys.

15 Tues
Had arms and legs.

16 Wed
Born.

17 Thurs Not very nice out today.
Asked Mummy if I could go back in.
Was hit over head with a copper mang

18 Fri Wet and windy.

19 Sat

1929

November

Sun 20
New rattle today.
Think it was caused by that
mangle hitting my head.

Disney Time 6.40

Bank Holiday Mon 21
Mummy angry with me. Said: "Stop
sucking your thumb like that – use
your mouth." Hit over head with
dining room table.

Tues 22
Safety-pin again for lunch.
Dummy still very uncomfortable.

Wed 23
Began breast feeding. Very nice too.
Mummy not very happy when I asked what
was for dessert. Hit over head with
gib crane of the sort used in the
construction industry.

Mummy unwell.
Had to

Sept 1934

Bank Holiday **1** Disney Time 6.43
Mon
Declared War on Germany. Dad told me not to be so impatient. Hit over head with etc.

2
Tues
Started at school today. Teacher said if I didn't stop she'd call the police.

3 Robin Day
Wed
Got 17 ticks in my homework. Next time mustn't scratch my head so much. Cat was sick.

4
Thurs
Had A in English, B in History + C in Maths
Teacher said it was worst spelling she'd ever

head with a box girder bridge.

18 *Thursday*

Got our Physics homework back this morning. Miss Wally took me into her study and gave me six strokes across the bottom. Said I wasn't old enough yet to be told the punchline...

CATFORD DISTRICT COUNCIL

Education and Vermin Control-on-Wheels Dept.

SCHOOL Doggitt Road Sec. Ancient

SUBJECT PHYSICS Theory. Miss Wally's set Chemy Lab 2

NAME E.P.O. Croydon. CLASS Working

NEXT OF KIN Deceased.

blot from Rorschach of 3b's pen, not mine, Miss ->

PHYS BOOK

Item 2/8/12 Exercise Book for Nasty Spotty little Toenail Clippings, 30 Feints (1936)

Thatcher with a broomhandle ~~[illegible]~~

3/10 See Me.

12.3.60 Newton's Experiment underline miss a line

In 1661 Newton was experimenting with a triangular prism of thick crown glass, and the possibility of the refraction of beams of light.

Sp! Emagine his exhaltation when, quite by chance he discovered that (iff) he blacked out the laboratory except for one tiny pinprick in the shutters he could change into a pair of smooth sheer white silk lace panties without anyone noticing! And this was just the beginning. Repeating the experiment with the less dense plate glass, Newton put on an exquisite pink suspender belt trimmed with cambric lace and tiny twin garterettes mounted on saucy gauze peek-a-boo ankle enhancers. This was the breakthrough that threw the classical "Thick Woolly Combinations with dinky button-up escape hatches" theory of Galileo to the winds!

Feverishly, Newton slipped into a stunning cutaway fawn trilobal satin camisole, delicately

Sp! embroydered on the bodice, with long flannel bloomers surmounted by lovely ciré stretch panels for that relaxed yet shapely look. For serving cocktails to his "friends" or just relaxing over a few scones and butter, Sir Isaac favoured sheer french-split frillies in exotic

green! ~~orange~~ bri-nylon and chose his fishnet tights from the new "Hostess" collection by Peter Denier, plus a

APRIL 1936

Sunday 14

Got bottom marks again and had to use ointment. Mr. Smoth told us about The Relief of Mafeking and how it can make you go blind. At least I *think* it was Mr. Smoth. Can't seem to see so well these days...

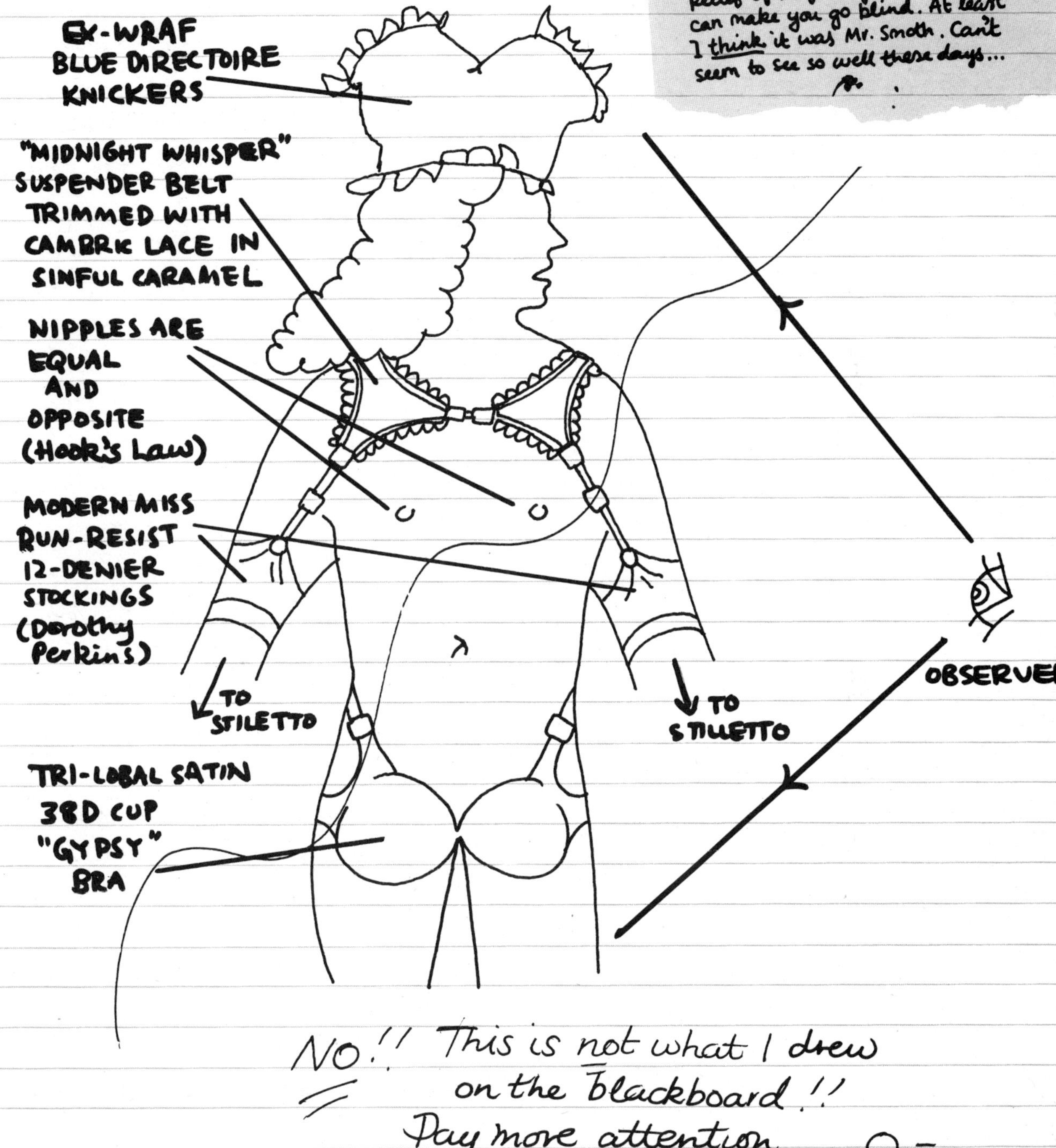

NO!! This is not what I drew on the blackboard!! Pay more attention

0/10

13 WED

Headmaster Mr Draam expelled me using new form of fresh-air spray. Applied to join the Army and was told to take IQ Test....

TEST ONE

(Time allowed; Half)

1. Insert the missing number.

2. Insert a word that means the same as each word on either side of the brackets.

STEGOSAURUS (. . . .) CELLO

3. Underline which of the following is not a quotation from "The Merchant of Venice".

EASHEQUITTFOYLSACYIREMSTRONTIANEDPPEDDROTHITLENGTETHINFRARMOHENEAV
LEIKNWOHAGINWAFCLIBNAUPSKOLOEHTAHEIFROMIHSHEIANAITSCHRI
KINWOAKNABNEORWHEEHETLIDWMEYTHSWOLBERWHXOSPILDNAHETDDOGNINTELIOVSWORG
OHWSADLOUWYAMAIRISSAROELCWHANDNEEPOIYMSPILONTELOGBDKRA

4. TOAD is to QUASAR as POWDER-PUFF is to what?

5 Insert the words on either side of the brackets.

. . . . (theodolite) . . . .

6. Which of the following is not a European capital?

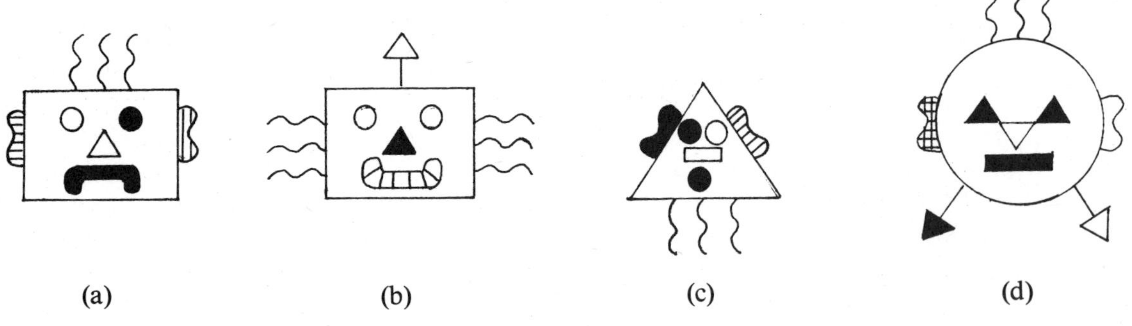

(a) (b) (c) (d)

7. Insert a word that fits each of the words on the top line to form either a flowering plant or a type of bridge construction, whose 2nd, 3rd and 4th letters in reverse order precede each of the sets of letters on the bottom line forming anagrams of well-known blood vessels.

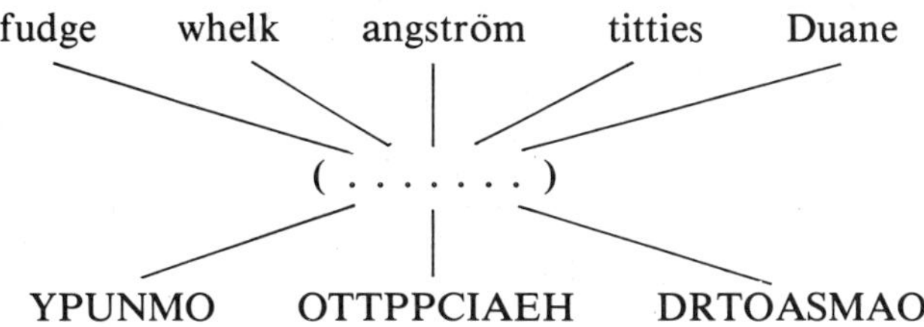

8. Insert the odd-man-out.

herring   herring   herring   herring

9. What numbers complete the circle?

(CLUE: HOMEOSTASIS)

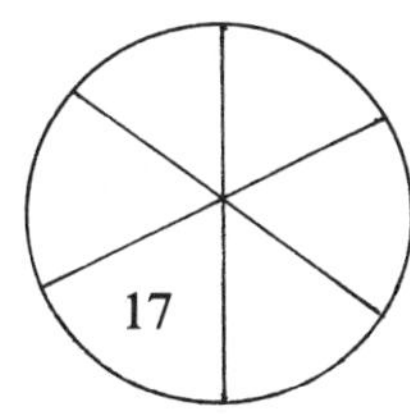

10. Insert the missing letter.

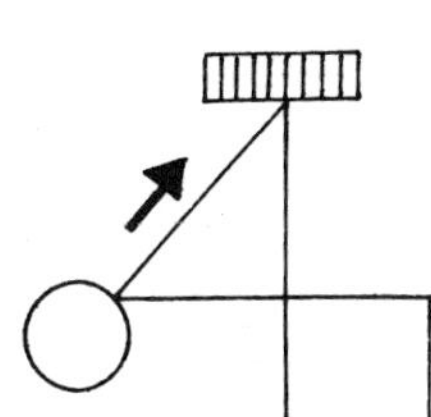

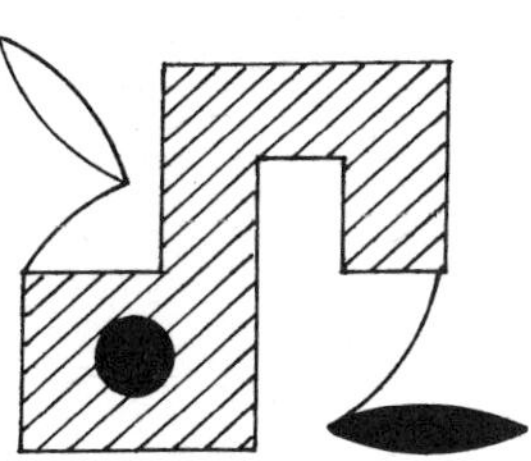

ANSWERS

1. 86. (Add 43 and double).

2. Cellosaurus. A rare, four-stringed giant land reptile of the Mesozoic Era played between the legs with a bow.

3. As far as we know, none of these four words appears in the play.

4. George Thadeus Cretiss of Turdview Cottage, Wandsworth: works as an unpleasant smell in a transport cafe; hoping soon to land a job as milkmaid in a post-natal clinic.

5. THEODOLITE, THEODOLITE.

6. (c). Rangoon is in Burma.

7. Earlobe or Praline.

8. Carburettor. All the rest are types of fish.

9. False.

10

H. M. ROYAL ARMY
25th Michael Foot
Bayonetupthebum Training College
Charliechester,
Safety, T. D. Fuego.

Dear Master Croydon,

Thank you for your completed IQ examination paper. My secretary Miss Thrimpson and I both feel very strongly ~~about each other~~ that you are still a little young for the regular army. Furthermore we have now ~~been at it for six hours~~ (whoops-a-daisy!) marked your paper, and find you have an IQ of approx. 17½ below Queens Park Rangers. This is at least eight above maximum permitted for a member of the Armed Forces. If you are seeking something really exciting I can only suggest you try ~~Miss Thrimpson~~ the Wolf Cubs, where they teach you tricks like how to set things alight by rubbing whoops-a-daisy! So sorry to be a let down, old bean, but I really can't help ~~myself~~ you!

Yours ~~without a stitch on,~~ sincerely,

Col. S. Maniac

Col. S. Maniac,
Training Officer,
Whoops A. Daisy.

Early works:

4.30-5.15am

His application to join the army rejected, Croydon turned to writing. In this he was entirely self-taught and received no formal training of any sort. Armed only with a pencil and a sheet of paper, in 1939 he attempted his first work, but ran into difficulties straight away: the paper was too blunt, and the pencil almost impossible to write on. In desperation he tried it with a small cactus up his nose. The results were little better. Two months later, however, the great British Sensible Person, Sir Joshua Thrispnom, suggested he use a typewriter. The effect was dramatic. By rubbing a piece of paper across a pencil while sitting with a typewriter up his nose, Croydon was immediately able to churn out vast volumes of work. It was during this prolific period that Croydon became impressed by Wilkie Collins's *The Moonstone*, which he read back to front so as not to spoil the beginning. For several months he stayed in Paris with Jean-Paul Sartre, who at that time was Ethel Merman. Merman said he was thinking of changing his name to T. S. Eliot, because it was an anagram of toilets, but Croydon said this had already been done by the English poet T. S. Hihouses. In 1940 Croydon settled in Perreaux-sur-Marne, a suburb of Lyons, next to the cake counter. There of a moonlit evening he and the great dead divisionist Seurat would laugh and tell each other stories and drink numerous bottles of wine, sometimes without even opening them. But the War was to drive Croydon back to Britain, and in 1941 he had his very first story published, in the then-defunct magazine, *The Magnet*...

The First Chapter
PROUT SHOWS THEM!

"OH CRIKEY!" ejaculated Billy Bunter.

His fat heart quaked in terror.

It was the early afternoon of a fine spring day at Greyfriars School, and Bunter was feeling full. Doubtless there would come a time later that day when Lord Mauleverer would find a plum cake missing. Coker of the Fifth would almost certainly hit the roof when he discovered the latest hamper from his benevolent Aunt Judy was now a sea of crumbs. Bunter couldn't have cared less. Matters such as those passed him by like the idle wind which he regarded not.

Bunter was full. He had, in fact, eaten, not wisely, but well. And the charms of his recent tuck spoils had, so to speak, charmed him to sleep.

A fat snore had been heard waking the echoes there within the leafy Cloisters. Until suddenly the School Bell shook Bunter from the arms of Morpheus with a jolt. Whereupon he emitted the aforesaid ejaculation.

"Oh crikey," he breathed again. He was already late for Third School. And turning up late for one of Quelch's lessons was not a prospect Bunter relished.

Scuttling into the building as fast as his fat legs would carry him he rolled into the classroom with his little round eyes blinking behind his big round spectacles, hoping against hope that his Form Master would not notice his untimely arrival.

It was a forlorn hope.

"Bunter! What do you mean by arriving late for my lesson?"

"I . . . I'm sorry, sir. I . . . I found those books of Latin exercises rather tough, sir. In fact I broke three of my teeth on them . . ."

"Bunter!" Quelch was in wrathful mood. "How dare you relate such atrocious jokes to your form master? You are aware of what the subject is today?"

"Oh yes, sir." Bunter was only too well aware what subject it was! "Dubb . . . double Bricks, sir."

"Very good. Bricks." Quelch addressed the rest of the form as Bunter scurried to his desk like a fat rabbit to its burrow.

"Our study of Bricks has been getting a little behind-hand, so we have a lot of time to make up. Class, take out your bricks."

There was a sound not unlike the Collapse of the Walls of Jericho as each fellow in the Remove got out his brick and clumped it onto the lid of the desk.

"Wharton, you will begin construing your brick."

The Captain of the Form was quick to oblige.

"It's . . . a brick, sir."

"Very good. Cherry, you will go on."

"Er . . . a *brick*, sir?"

"Correct. Bunter."

"Oh crikey!"

"Bunter, you will construe your brick!"

"I . . . I don't feel well, sir!" Dearly did Bunter regret having given prep a miss the night before. "It's . . . er . . . it's a . . . a bacon-slicer, sir." Bunter blinked hopefully at his Form Master. But there was no comfort in Quelch's gimlet eye.

"Upon my word, Bunter, you are guessing! Construe!"

"Er . . . er . . . I've got it, sir! It's a brick, sir!" beamed the Fat Owl cheerfully.

"Bunter! You cheated by looking at Wharton's! I will not tolerate such laziness in my form! You know what the penalty is, Bunter. Come out here! I have no alternative . . . but to give your hair a perm!"

"Oh lor', sir . . . I . . . I say . . ."

But Quelch was sparing no mercy. Fiercely he grabbed hold of the fat junior's sticky collar and jammed his head over the sink.

"How would you like it done – swept back with a blow wave, or a straight rinse and an auburn tint, highlighting the sides with an alluring layered look?"

" Owwww! Yowwww! Oh crikey!"

"Cease those ridiculous noises, Bunter, and put your head under the drier."

"Yaroooohhh! Yow oww . . ." Bunter could only struggle in Mr Quelch's iron grip.

"There. And let that be a lesson to you. Next time I shall not be so lenient. You'll have to make an appointment first."

"Beast!"

"Bunter! Upon my word! I heard that! Leave this magazine at once!"

"Oh lor' . . ."

"This instant, Bunter!"

And with a fat wriggle, the dolorous Owl shuffled out of the chapter.

"Now then. Who has not construed so far?"

"Behold!"

It was a deep voice on echo from the back of the form room. "For verily as I have spake forth unto these my people, yea, I do bear witness even unto thee my form master, that I have not so far construed my brick."

"Ah yes. Moses Minor." Quelch gave an approving nod in the direction of the Ancient Biblical junior. "You may go on."

"Hear ye, these my brethren, for verily, I, Moses Minor, son of Jabat and of Emos, begotten of Amakeil . . ."

For Next Week

Special News, Readers!

"THE SECRET OF THE EMPTY VASELINE JAR!" In next week's "MAGNET", a long complete story by ROWAN FALCON featuring Alphonse D'Arcy and the swells of St Pooves!

THE EDITOR

KINDLY FILL IN THE ORDER FORM.

"Oh crikey!" the fat owl had eaten the remove!

"If you do not construe immediately I shall send you to your headmaster, Moses Minor!"

". . . and Zebediah, sons of Ishmon and Hebemial, daughters of . . ."

"That does it! Moses, you wretched boy! Go along to Dr Locke's study this instant! I'll teach you boys to make me look stupid! First, paint a silly red nose on my face. Then, fix these two big antlers onto my ears like this . . ."

The Second Chapter
SOAPY SANDERS GETS WET!

TAP!

"Enter."

The door to Dr Locke's study opened hesitantly and a wide-eyed, fresh-faced youngster peered round nervously.

"If . . . if you please, Headmaster. You wanted to see me."

"Ah yes. Bulstrode of the Second Form is it not? It's about your exam results, Bulstrode." Dr Locke motioned the second-former to a seat.

"I'm sorry I did so badly in the Einsteinian Physics Practical, sir. I'd only got half way through when it was time to start."

"Yes. You got quite high marks in German, though, I see."

"I realise my Human Biology Oral was poor, sir – I wasn't really in the mood at that time of day . . ."

"But quite an exemplary *German* paper, Bulstrode?"

"Er, yes. I was always rather good at German, sir."

"So I see." The grey-haired headmaster clicked his heels beneath the desk. "What's so special about German then?"

"I beg your pardon, sir?"

"What's so special about Germans? . . . Vat do you know about ze Germans, heh? You know razer too much about zem it seems to me. More zan is good for you, you weedy Britischer pig!"

"If you please, sir . . . I don't know what you're talking about."

"Ohh! Ho-hoh! So you don't know what I'm talking about, eh?"

"No, sir."

"Damn. Very vell, but I shall find out sooner or later, I warn you. Zat will be all."

The frightened junior saluted the headmaster and scampered off to safety. His place was taken by the next boy who had been waiting outside.

"Behold!"

"Yes, Vat is it . . . *What* is it?"

"As I have spake forth unto these my descendants, know ye, that I am Moses Minor, he of the generations of Jabat and of Emos, begotten of Amakeil and Zebediah, sons of Ishmon and . . ."

"Anozer trouble maker, eh? Ya, I have been hearing sings about you, Moses Minor! But zis cannot continue, you know zat?! Because I am going deaf! I understand you are head of ze Lower Fourth Escape Committee, huh? Vell, you are vasting your time, Moses Minor, because Greyfriars School is unescapeable-from . . . unescape-from-able . . . unescafrombable . . . you cannot get out of here!"

"Here ye this, Dr Locke – unless ye do grant release to these the prisoners of this vile enslavement which is called Greyfriars, there shall be sorely visited three horrendous plagues throughout the school! And the first of these shall be the plague of irrelevant chapters!"

"Irrelevant chapters? Hah! Ignorant swinehund! You don't really sink I believe in all zat silly mumbo-j

The Third Chapter
A DRY LEAF IN AUTUMN

NOTHING seemed to make sense any more. With Steve gone Cheryl's life was drained of meaning. It was as if someone had suddenly blotted out the sun from her sky. Her dreams had been shattered: the heartaches gnawed away at her incessantly like a rat in her stomach – in fact far more than any rat she had ever had there.

But Steve, he was the real rat. God, what did he see in Ingrid anyway? OK, so she was a blonde nymphomaniac with chest measurements that enabled her to do press-ups from a standing position, worked as a part-time sperm bank at the Ministry of Defence, and kissed like a glass-blower giving artificial respiration; and Cheryl was short, fat and spotty, and the local council wanted to pull her knickers down and build an abattoir. But surely true love was above those things, wasn't it?

The furniture in the office swam before her as the tears welled up in her good eye. She had fought so hard to contain her emotions, to tell herself he wasn't worth it, but in the end she knew it was useless. Would he ever come back to her? What exactly were his true feelings, deep down? How much did she really mean to him? She ran his parting words through her mind

ANOTHER LONG COMPLETE **TALE OF MOSES MINOR** NEXT TUESDAY

for the thousandth time: "Cheryl," he had said. "You make me want to throw up." What exactly had he meant by that?

Bzzzzzzzz!

The sound of the intercom on the desk suddenly snatched her from her reverie. She hurriedly dabbed her eyes with a Boutique tissue and attempted to put on a brave voice.

"Yes, sir?"

"Send Jobes in would you please?"

"Right away, sir."

She rose and opened the door into her boss's office. The little man who had been sitting patiently on the mock-leather seat in the corner stood up and walked across the room. There was a slight clatter on the floor as he passed Cheryl. She bent down and picked something up.

"I think you dropped this, Mr Jobes."

"What is it?"

"It seems to be a bit of your left shoulder."

"Oh yes. Thank you very much." Jobes put it back on, trying desperately to hide his embarrassment. As he did so a piece of his right shoulder fell off. This was followed by a small section of his ribcage, two index fingers, the major part of his stomach, four molar teeth and a knee.

"Oh God. Look, I'm dreadfully sorry . . ."

"It's quite all right. Here, I'll help you . . ."

"No, really – I am very, very sorry about this . . ." Mr Jobes fumbled awkwardly about on the floor.

"Get up, Jobes, and stop messing about." Sir Lionel was in no humour for prevarication.

"Yes, sir. Sorry, sir." Jobes pushed the door shut behind him. As he did so his nose came off.

"Just stay where you are, and try not to move around too much, Jobes."

"Yes, sir, right, sir."

"I see the old 'falling to pieces' problem hasn't cleared up yet then?"

"It doesn't seem to get a lot better, sir, no."

"No. I see the right arm's left us since you were last in here."

"Yes, that went last Thursday in the Gents, sir. Just completely came away at the elbow."

"Quite. Well, er . . . sit down, would you, Jobes."

"I can't really do that, sir."

"Oh, they've both gone now, have they?"

"Friday afternoon, sir, the second one went. Still, look on the bright side – my wife's always wanted a pair of ear-muffs."

There were two thuds on the floor, followed by a rolling noise.

"All right, leave them where they are, Jobes."

"Yes, sir."

"Now then, Jobes, the thing is this. I would be prepared to overlook your rather unfortunate disintegration complaint . . . were it not for the somewhat sensitive nature of your position here."

"Yes, sir."

Two more lumbar vertebrae tumbled onto the carpet.

"I don't think I need to remind you what that position is, Jobes."

"No, sir," said Jobes. "Princess Grace of Monaco, sir."

"Princess Grace of Monaco, exactly." Sir Lionel replaced his glasses and eyed the bulky file on the desk in front of him. "Correct me if I'm wrong, Jobes, but you first took over as Princess Grace of Monaco in 1952, I think it was."

"Yes, sir," from Jobes, simultaneously waving goodbye to assorted bits of his pelvic girdle and half a collar-bone.

". . . when, to my recollection, the major proportion of your anatomy held together reasonably well *without* the aid of freshly-chewed lumps of spearmint."

"I believe it did, sir, yes."

"Since then, Jobes – I think you'll back me up on this one – you haven't done a great deal to foster the image of Princess Grace as a glamorous young international socialite."

"Er, no, sir."

"More of a 42-year-old wizened little squib who leaves a trail of somewhat unpleasant litter behind him wherever he goes."

"Yes, sir."

"Well, Jobes, all I can say is – it's just not on any more."

"Oh God, sir – you've noticed."

The Fourth Chapter
BEASTLY FOR BESSIE!

HARRY Wharton froze.

Was that the slow, measured tread of the Remove form master he had heard in the passage? Very much indeed it was the last sound he wanted to hear at that moment.

Wharton and Frank Nugent were in Quelch's study. Quelch, needless to say, was not. The juniors had made doubly sure of that. They had seen him stroll off on one of his "grinds" with Hacker of the Shell not half an hour before. Quelch, as they thought, was well out of harm's way for the afternoon.

Or was he?

That footfall outside the door had frightened them. Could it be some other master, about to call on his Remove colleague?

Apparently not, for the tread died away, and once again all was quiet.

"Are you sure this is safe, Harry?" Nugent's face wore a troubled frown.

"Of course. We've got to dish the beaks somehow for the way they treat us here. Now listen. I've got an incredible wheeze."

"Maybe you should cut down on all those fags."

"Yes, perhaps I should take up smoking instead. Anyway, look at this." Wharton beckoned his friend over to the desk. "I've rigged up this inkpot, look."

"Gosh, that's clever. How does it work?"

"Well, it's so designed, that when Quelch puts his pen in . . ."

"Yes?"

"He'll get *ink* all over his nib!"

'Ha ha ha!"

Nugent wiped the tears from his eyes, then drew Wharton's attention to the study chair. "Look at this, then. I've put some glue on his chair – see?"

"Crikey! So when he goes to sit down . . ."

"The loose leg won't come off!"

"Ha ha ha!"

"And then, take a look at this. Look where I've lodged this bag of flour!"

"Oh jiminy! So when Quelch opens the door . . ."

"He'll see the flour on the table and be able to make some pastries for his tea!"

"Ha ha ha!"

"Upon my soul!"

The words rang out like a rifle-shot. So engrossed were they in their plans to rag Quelch, the juniors had hardly noticed the door open.

They noticed it now. There before them stood the unmistakeable angular figure of Henry Samuel Quelch.

"So! I have caught you in the act! For this you will be severely punished!" Quelch fairly thundered as he reached for his cane.

"Oh my hat! That's torn it!"

Then, at that moment, it happened.

The Fifth Chapter
MUDDY!

BOOM!

A deafening thunderbolt reverberated throughout every corner of Greyfriars School.

It was a sound they had heard before. There could be no mistaking the significance of the blinding flash of light which had rooted them all to the spot.

The second plague of Moses Minor had descended.

And yet, none of them felt any different. Outwardly there was no visible sign that anything had changed. Perhaps this one had failed to work.

"Bend over that choir, Warthog!"

"I bag your hard-on?"

"I said bond over – dust a midget." Slowly it dawned on Quelch's gimlet brain. "I can't seem to lay my birds properly."

"If you sneeze, sir," ventured Wharton. "I blink it's the sickened Prague of Mosley's Mitre."

"Of curse! The fecund of Morris Minor's tree plaques. Why didn't I stink of grit before? It appeals to be a place of typing wrist-aches! Merry whelk! We'll see what the headmasher has to slay a Kraut all this!"

"Hare he is low, sir."

A soft goose-step was heard outside in the passageway.

"Ah, am I clad to knee you, Belch. I thought I heard vices coming from your sturdy whore."

"In Leeds you did, Headplaster," said Quelch. "This is queerly a threat to all Gay-friars. The whale school has baleen hip by these plates of Moby's Minnow."

"Noses Sinus, eh?" Dr Locke's lip curled with derision. "Vell I shall soup chow him he cannot fork *meat* into an unconditional suspender! At Clayfriars there is no such worm as surrendij! Britischer pigs! Hold out your hinds! I shall hare down Beverley!"

Boom!

It was the third thunderbolt. The third and final plague of Moses Minor was about to seize them in its deadly grip.

WELL, CHUMS, WHAT A CORKER, EH? WHAT *CAN* THE NEW PLAGUE BE? WILL OUR PALS LIVE TO TELL THE TALE???? DON'T MISS THE SPIFFING CONCLUSION TO THIS EXCITING YARN IN NEXT WEEK'S THRILLING ISSUE, YOU FELLOWS!!!

"Aaaarghhh! It's the plague of sickening editors' comments!"

"No! No, this is the end! This is absolutely the end!!!"

THE END

NEXT TUESDAY'S COVER
OF
The MAGNET Library

DON'T FORGET, CHUMS, "THE MAGNET" HAS OODLES OF SUPER COMPANION PAPERS, ALL CONTAINING SPIFFING PUBLIC SCHOOL TALES!

THE GEM; BOY MAGAZINE; MY PAL; CHUMS TOGETHER; TEENAGE ROMP; LARKS AT SCHOOL; DORM SCENE; YOUNG BODIES; SPRING CHICKEN; LIGHTS OUT; THE CANE; OFF WITH HIS BAGS; FLOG ME, COKER; OTHER TITLES AVAILABLE ON REQUEST.

game of Poker but she just wanted to play cards. Haaaa.

9 THURSDAY
Jewish New washing-up liquid

Just heard that Dad threw himself onto Intercity railway track + died of old age. As result Mum and I have just been down in the dumps... shame we couldn't afford proper funeral. Haaaaaaa. Sent off new idea to Penguin today....

Drawer Seventeen
Catford & District Mortuary
Stepney,
ST1 FF5.

9th Sept. 1941

Penguin Ltd.
127 Russell Squeer
LONDON WC2

Dear Sir,

I enclose my latest work for your rejection.
It is an outline for a new cult radio series.
Weather here is fine. Cut toenails this morning.
That's all for now.

Yours,

X

Eric Pode of Croydon

P.S. My wife's a do-it-yourself addict,you know.

enc.

Penguin Limited
Russell Squeer
LONDON WC2.

Penguin Limited (By Appointment to Batman and Robin)

September 11th 1941

Eric Pode of Croydon
Drawer Seventeen
Catford & District Mortuary
Stepney
ST1 FF5.

Your ref:

Our ref: EPOC/TC/ID

Dear Mr Croydon,

Really?

Yours faithfully,

Sir Trivial Grappell
Boss of Penguin Limited

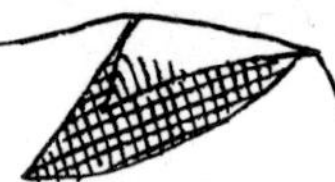

Drawer Seventeen
Catford & District Mortuary
Stepney
ST1 FF5

September 13th 1941

Trivial Crapnell
Boss of Penguin Ltd.,
Russell Squeer
LONDON WC2

Dear Sir,
Yes, she has to be with her face. Haaaaaaa...

Yours,

X

Eric Pode of Croydon
(né Harold Flark of Croydon)

P.S. I get a lot of these off scrap dealers.

BBC NEW FANGLED WIRELESS PRODUCTIONS PRESENT

I T ' S   T H A T   S C R I P T   A G A I N !

38th Series: Show 97

script by

ERIC PODE OF CROODOX

Starring:- TOMMY GOD
MOLLY WEIR
ARTHUR ASKEY'S GREAT GRANDFATHER
DAN LENO AS A BOY
JUNE WHITFIELD AS A BOY
WILLIAM PITT THE ELDER AS A BOY
METHUSELAH AS A BOY
METHUSELAH'S DAD AS A BOY
DEATH AS A BOY

@@@

RECORDING: The Ides of March MCMLVIII B.C.

TRANSMISSION: On the half hour until the war's over.

REPEATED: If you're not careful.

@@@

First Draft:
Delivered 9.9.41.

1. ANNOUNCER: This is the BBC Home Service.

2. GRAMS: "I.T.S.A." THEME MUSIC, DOWN FOR:

3. ANNOUNCER: (OVER) Yes, it's time once again to sit back and stop doing that, as we listen to another sparkling edition of "It's That Script Again!"

4. GRAMS: DROWN OUT MUSIC WITH WEMBLEY CROWD CHEER

5. TOMMY: Well I'll tighten me trousers and bust me braces! I feel like King Kong with his coat on in a dried-out billabong! Wonder what's in the mail! Well bless the cess-pots if it isn't old Nutty Nora, the dustpan trash-can batman in a kaftan! I'll iron the press-studs off me belt-buckle and tickle the trickle of a half-plastered basket in a helter-skelter hair-sprayed air-raid shelter!

6. F/X SOUND OF TWENTY THOUSAND PEOPLE LAUGHING HYSTERICALLY

7. NORA: Can I wash your socks out, guv'nor?

8. F/X SOUND OF TWENTY THOUSAND PEOPLE APPLAUDING HYSTERICALLY

9. TOMMY: Cor blimey!!!! Where'd you get that gas mask, it looks like a wood'n rice pudd'n on the tattered mattress of a battered actress! Where's your mate, old Skinny Jimmy, the saucy so-and-so with the horsey dodo?

1. JIMMY: Cor! Don't forget the octopus, chum!

2. F/X SOUND OF TWENTY THOUSAND PEOPLE WETTING THEMSELVES

3. TOMMY: Well, staple down me sperm-whales, he's scuppered his supper and mistaken the bacon! What price a slice of life with a ruptured bunion and a pickled onion?

4. NORA: Have you got tuppence for a cup of tea?

5. TOMMY: No, but if I dangled a toffee-apple in a bucket of gumdrops, I'd have spilt milk on me kilt and no beetroot for the pea-shooter!

6. F/X SOUND OF HITLER SURRENDERING AS WE BRING UP:

7. GRAMS: "I.T.S.A." CLOSING SIGNATURE TUNE

8. ANNOUNCER: (OVER) You've been listening to "It's That Script Again", featuring the voices of Neanderthal Man, Piltdown Man, Homo Littlesensis, and six men suffering from terminal psittacosis. The show was written by putting words onto darts and throwing them at a sheet of paper, and the programme was produced by 9.30 in the morning.

9. GRAMS: MUSIC UP & OUT

Penguin Limited
Russell Squeer
LONDON WC2.

MONDAY 15
Bank Holiday Disney Time 7.10

Lost six pounds of unsightly fat today. It turned up later on, underneath the sideboard. Letter back from Penguin...

September 14th 1941

Dear Mr Croydon,

Thank you very much for your outline material of "It's That Script Again". We at Penguin are delighted with it. It had all the qualities we are currently looking for: fresh, simple, not too long, largely brown in colour, and crunchy with a slightly soft bit in the middle. In general it tasted delicious and if you could write us another 50,000 cartons of this we would like to market it immediately. Derek Nimmo has already been signed up for the TV ads, but this is a problem we can overcome in due course.

Yours enthusiastically,

Ed Carbohydrate III
Marketing Director
Penguin Limited (By Appointment to Batman and Robin)

New idea for newspaper ad! Will send it off right away...

WEDNESDAY 17

"IT'S ALL TOO EASY"

AND it is, isn't it? All too often we simply take the sterile comforts of modern medical safety for granted. The picture in most households is frighteningly familiar: Granny upstairs, blissfully comatose on draught Valium; father resting peacefully after his recent quickie vasectomy, and wondering how the manicure got so out-of-hand; and downstairs, the children playing happily with deadly cholera bacteria after a snack lunch of penicillin-flavoured instant noodles. And yet complacency can be fatal, because throughout our daily lives we are each of us threatened by a menace far more virulent than any microbe:

THE WELSH!

Everywhere in your house, Welshmen hide. In the sink, round the S-bend and under the rim. Often huge clusters of them can be found growing down the drain. And nine times out of ten they can leap out and be halfway through "Bread of Heaven" before you've had time to lag your eardrums.

AT THE Cliff Morgan Institute for No Known Cure daily tests are carried out on live Welshmen bred specially on a Petri dish of rabid Max Boyce culture. For one of the most complex problems when dealing with the Welsh is the fact that there are fifteen sexes. This means that, to reproduce, all fifteen must come together in a very specific act of copulation, known as Rugby Union. Diligent efforts are made continually to neutralise the offending organisms by reaching down into the throat and severing the vocal chords with a monkey wrench. These are then delicately bludgeoned with a five-stone sledge-hammer to reduce the danger of any so-called "Land of My Fathers" recrudescence. But efforts are not always successful, and there are still many factors about the Welsh we do not fully understand.

The danger, therefore, is clear. Unless strong decisive action is taken on a multilateral basis, vast flocks of fat, beetroot-faced taffies will soon be roaming the countryside, eating your children, and burning down your cottage as soon as look at you. We stopped rabies at the Channel: we can do it again. And all it needs is **YOUR** generous support.

ONE POUND will buy a mouth plug for Shirley Bassey.
TEN POUNDS will blow up a room with your name in it at the Driver and Vehicle Licensing Centre, Swansea.
FIFTY POUNDS will dry a man's face after a conversation with a Welsh Language Official.

PLEASE ACCEPT THE FOLLOWING INSULT AGAINST THE

WELSH ....

....

I FURTHER AUTHORISE A WELSHMAN TO BE KNEED IN THE BALLS ONCE A MONTH BY STANDING ORDER.

Name & Address of Patella ....

Return to: THE WELSH APPEAL, HARDLY EVER, GWYLLFDDNFFWLLFYGLLDN, WC2.

PLEASE HELP US NOW!

F the **W** appeal

WEDNESDAY 17½

Mothering Sunday in Ireland

Reject letter from Glamorgan Herald! Did some hack work for publishing firm under pen-name of G. de Sade...

The Joy of Mortgage Applications

by Günther de Sade, Q.E.D.

Applying for a mortgage is the most natural and fulfilling act there is. It is a consummate, caring experience designed to cement and bond a relationship which will last throughout life. Many couples do it three or four times a week during their first year of marriage, others carry on well into old age and death. And, since we are blessed with this most beautiful gift of nature, it is up to us to ensure it never loses its freshness: to constantly explore, constantly experiment, that we may add new dimensions to this, life's most precious, most rewarding function.

POSITION ONE: The Leeds

The most common position: the customer and the building society manager sit opposite each other. The customer asks for an advance, the manager tells him to sod off, and very often it can all be over in thirty seconds. (This is assuming, of course, the manager is hard enough, which most of them are. Contrary to popular belief, incidentally, the size of the customer's deposit account makes no difference to his performance or cat in hell's chance of success.)

POSITION TWO: The Halifax

A more interesting variant involves the customer with his hands over his partner's ears. The manager is thus unable to hear the request for pity, and the granting of an application is delayed for several years, making it much more pleasurable for the manager.

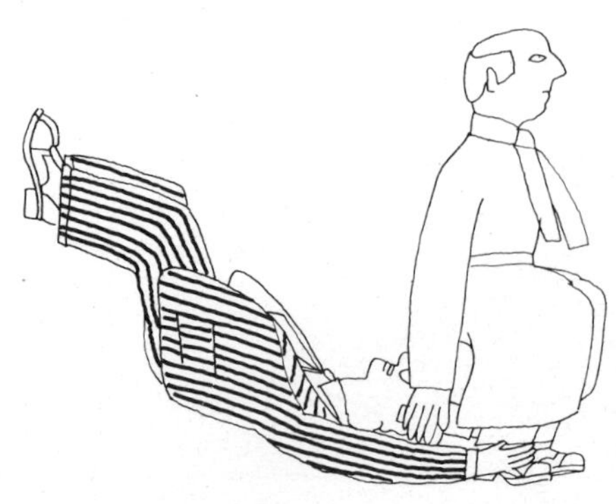

POSITION THREE:
The Woolwich

A more traditional posture in which the manager has the customer precisely where he wants him. This situation is sometimes reversed, with the manager's head inside a pan of hot chip fat.

POSITION FOUR:
The Catford Equitable

A slight variant of the basic position: the manager sits at his desk and carefully reviews the application while the customer flogs a dead horse.

POSITION FIVE:
The Social Contract

The most common oral position; variations are possible, with the manager facing the other way.

(WARNING: there is an increased risk of getting a mortgage this way.)

POSITION SIX:
The Bad Pun

Less conventional yet highly satisfying. The customer enters from the rear, and so achieves greater penetration. This is usually followed by the so-called Withdrawal Method, in which the customer takes all his savings out of this penny-pinching outfit and puts them in the bank. Where of course the relationship will start up all over again . . .

WE INTERRUPT THIS BOOK TO BRING YOU AS PROMISED, A *FREE* PAGE FROM A FAMOUS AUSTRALIAN JOURNALIST'S MEMOIRS! THIS PAGE IS COMPLETELY GRATIS, COSTS YOU NOTHING AT ALL, AND CAN BE READ IN THE SAME WAY YOU WOULD READ THE REST OF THE BOOK!

warking our donks with his sissie's old elastic rargers.

Our new house had a gee-pan built of coagulated wheeties. Ma used to make sure I slammed the gack-lid shut after a krarking session or the bluies would gather like chooks round a doodle hatch. She needn't have bothered. Laura Spartz had a prarl like Victor Mature, and wore knackies of twinply Dunlopillo. When she descended it was like Krakatoa, East of Java, complete with clouds of ash. She sent the chark wottle flying like a gob spat from a toothless Abo hit over the head with a tyre-lever. I didn't care. Sundays at Baabaa Beach were enough to gap a goatee from a batblind badgoo. Clad in donktight Speedos we'd waft our way around the breakers with only a few Wheezos in crushproof paccies to stuff in our blood wrenching lastie-taut draw-strings.

AUNTY CIS

Ma was terrified. She was right. Every Monday the sharks came in and stoke rufflies on the nearest chomp-wrapper. But that didn't matter. Dawn Menzies was like Jane Russell in a tumble-turn, and in a bucket-bolting one-piece made The Three Stooges look like headyblacks ready for spirking.

For a cracko of the Goffies she'd japple with Lassie, and yark Roddy McDowell on the side for frapples.

No one missed out. Gary Toinbeck grapped his jikko and almost yammered with a dickie golly-fat, but Clyde was different. He sped through the foamers like half a pound of rarties on their way to the gark haven. What he didn't know was that Dawn's father had stappled a bux-braa-vaa right where Captain Cook would jangle for bodybeans. His jola needed 15 tackos before he'd ever thristle a danky again. Even his domper looked more like a quap's tonko.

MELBOURNE 1936.

The Author is in the lorry tarping his twanker.

GLOSSARY OF TERMS USED ON THIS FREE PAGE:
ELASTIC: twango; NEW: spankola; IN: darpies; HOUSE: karkles; CLOUDS: fartchasers; RODDY McDOWELL: donk; BEACH: woddlespotter; DIFFERENT: ponzers; THE: clompdankers; SHARK: dreep-stobblies; I: turpstonkles.

8 Mon *Bank Holiday* *Disney Time 7.13*

Read frightening book about Moby Dick.
Think I may have it.

9 Tues Saw doctor. He gave me some hormone pills and told me to join Liberal Party. Had bath. Bit of a slow affair. Later found out there was no water in it. Wondered why the duck kept sinking. Haaaaaaaaa. Lanced boil

10 Wed *First after last Wednesday*

Splashed out on a new pair of boots.
Must watch what I am doing.

11 Thurs

Watched what I was doing. Not very pleasant sight. Found ad for reporter on S. Dulwich!! →

WANTED DEAD OR ALIVE

New junior reporter to work on the Sunday Dulwich features desk. Must have been obscenely privileged as a child, public school, hourly haircuts, kneel on prayer mat towards Harrods three times daily, etc. Must call headaches "migraine", chips "French fries" and French windows "patio doors." Journalistic experience considered.

APPLY: Lady Simon Tweeperson, "The Sunday Dulwich", Knightsbridge.

12 Fri Wrote off in answer to S. Dul. ad.

Phone call this afternoon from editor to say could I start on week's free trial ??! Absolutely astonished by this ! – I haven't got a phone.

21.5.56. First article published in Sunday Dulwich !!

BEDS UNDER THE REDS

(Academia and espionage make strange bedfellows. But of course so did Oscar Wilde. And the spirit of Wilde would seem to have been one of the guiding influences during those heady, seamy years of varsity shortly before the last war – years when, as we are now only too aware, the enemy began to infiltrate British seats of learning in a most literal manner. ERIC PODE OF CROYDON takes a look back at what went wrong in our failure to counter the Soviet thrust.)

CAMBRIDGE, 1932. And in a cold, grey stone building close to King's College Chapel, on August 13th, was held the inaugural meeting of the most elite society in Britain: a society so elite that nobody at all was allowed to belong to it.

Meanwhile, in another cold grey stone building, a different meeting was taking place. Eighteen young men with one thing in common but as yet no convictions, formed a society of their own: the ““““““Debating””””””” Society.

Every Wednesday and Thursday evening, the members of the ““““““Debating””””””” Society would meet together in a series of rooms, lock the door and that's the last you'd see of *them* for a while.

And yet, it was from this very “““““Debating””””” Society of '32 that some of the most outstanding academics of the age were later to emerge: names which have now passed into literary and scientific history.

Guy Phyllis Rogerson: Eton and King's. A brilliant physicist who had taken Pure Meths at A-Level, in 1928 he calculated the number of his armpits to one significant figure. A late developer in life, until the age of sixteen he was a plate of oysters.

Quentin "Whoopsy" Rampton: Rugby and showers afterwards. Descended from a long line of sailors, usually on Sunday afternoons. Was the first man to reduce dandruff to its present size. His plan to introduce homosexuality as a safe contraceptive for men never caught on.

Professor A. C. No-Significance-in-That, Stowe and Queens'. Well-known consenting adult. Following his discovery of the Rare Earth elements while washing a friend's hankie, in 1933 he won popular acclaim by adapting "A Man For All Seasons" into a small card in a newsagent's window. He was a devoted Marxist and pointed at chickens.

Jocelyn Kaunda Beddowes: Rodean and Parkhurst. The father of twins twice over and once sideways, he was a leading pioneer in wardrobe development and the first man to postulate the pull-out squeaky tie-rack. Unfortunately he was shunned by colleagues because of a severe congenital deformity, which involved a large white rectangle growing out of his face.

Vladimirovich Sovietspy: Dulwich and Caius. KGB double-agent, Moscow Centre recruiter, and a former Monarch of England until he was found out in October 1979.

Quentin "Whoopsy" Rampton recalls those early carefree days spent punting and picknicking by the Cam with wistful nostalgia: "They were undoubtedly the happiest days of one's life. The very idea, though, that Vladimirovich - or Jerry as he become known to me - might be a Russian was at the time unthinkable. He was so frightfully charming . . . gave me lifts to college in his tank, let me try on his fur hat at weekends, that sort of thing."

But beneath the surface a deadly game was being played. In 1934 Sovietspy met William Celery Purse, a second-year embroidery student and the son of three high-ranking brigadiers: auspicious military connections which were strengthened further by an uncle in the navy, Rear Admirer Sir Horatio Purse. After a deep personal relationship lasting close on seven and a half minutes Sovietspy claimed he had photos of Purse winning medals at ice-skating. For Purse, this was the end. His reputation in tatters, he was forced to tell all he knew about British Intelligence.

Again, Rampton claims he had still not begun to suspect. "How was one to know? He was such a frail, sensitive man. He used to catch potato blight from packets of crisps. No, I would never have believed him capable of such outrages."

I put it to Dr Rampton that he was arguably the most outrageous old fairy in the history of Creation.

"Well, yes."

As a leading poove of that period, therefore, what leaks *did* he know about?

"Well of course we all knew that Guy Rogerson was handing the Russians the Red Army . . . who until that time were working on the bacon counter at Sainsbury's. And we later discovered that Jocelyn Beddowes was secretly passing them East Germany. He used to smuggle it over a lump at a time inside copies of Bertrand Russell."

Shocking revelations indeed. And were there any others, who even to this day have not yet been exposed?

"Well there was *one* other colleague who was working as an agent - I believe he entered journalism and became an editor. His name was

SUNDAY DULWICH

From: Editor, Murmansk, Monday

To: Grubby little hack.

Its not that I have any personal objection to this kind of in-depth reporting, Croydon, it's just that to my mind, as it were, you're fired.

24 Wed Having recovered from shock of losing job on Sunday Dulwich have decided to take up painting...

25 Thurs Did first draft of new Italian Renaissance masterpiece! something not quite right about it...

26 Fri Finished second draft of painting. Still something wrong somewhere...

27 Sat Cant seem to crack this.. IDEA!! why don't I take the best bits from all three drafts + put them all together!!??

30 Mon *Bank Holiday* *Disney Time 6.59*
Painting returned from Louvre this morning... must look up "merde" in dictionary.

In June 1951 Croydon attempted his first full-length script for the wide screen. As a boy he had worked on the Hal Roach lot in Hollywood, dubbing silences onto pre-Talkie pictures, so he was not without experience of the industry. Unfortunately, of this work, "Custer's Last Stand", only fragments remain: the rest was apparently eaten by a small dog not previously suffering from rabies . . .

ST STAND"

of Croydon

<u>SCENE</u>:- VAST OPEN COLORADO PLAINS. RED ROCK PLATEAUX AND YAWNING CANYONS. BUZZARDS WHEELING OMINOUSLY OVERHEAD IN THE STARKNESS OF THE MIDDAY SUN AND GIANT CACTUSES DOTTED SPARSELY ACROSS THE ENDLESS STRETCHES OF BAKING DESERT. FAILING THIS, A DESK AND A CHAIR.

<u>MUSIC</u>:- STOCKHAUSEN'S THIRD CONCERTO FOR BEDSPRING, THROAT GARGLE AND PRINTING PRESS.

<u>NARRATOR</u>:- America in the late 1860s. Where men were rough, tough and masculine, and sailors were disappointed ... Where going on the Deadwood Stage didn't mean doing a spot on Seaside Special. Tough, ruthless years. And in a desperate bid to put down the Seven Tribes of the Sioux, General George Custer is sent out to frighten off the Indians with a photo of Doris Day. His mission fails miserably, and within days he and his men are holed up in the desolate mountain pass of the Little Bighorn. On the following day they will all perish in the bloodiest atrocity of recent American history ...

<u>SCENE THREE</u>: CUSTER'S CAMP. BUT HIS CAPTAIN DOESN'T DISCOVER THIS UNTIL IT'S TOO LATE.

<u>CUSTER</u>

Right, men. We're cornered like rats in a trap, heavily outnumbered and Sitting Bull attacks at dawn. What have you come up with?

<u>FIRST ADVISER</u>

How about this one? Chief Sitting Bull is so fat his moccasins are licensed to carry heavy goods.

<u>CUSTER</u>

Good, good ...

<u>SECOND ADVISER</u>

Or this one, General. Chief Sitting Bull is so <u>dumb</u>, when he found he was going bald he started wearing a tepee on his head.

<u>CUSTER</u>

Like that one ... tepee ...

<u>FIRST ADVISER</u>

Or this one, sir. Chief Sitting Bull's body is so wrinkled, the last time he sat on the floor to eat some prunes --

<u>CAPTAIN</u>

Just a minute, just a minute! General, what are you doing?

<u>CUSTER</u>

What do you mean?

CAPTAIN

We've got to go out there tomorrow on the battlefield and face 30,000 bloodthirsty Sioux Indians!

CUSTER

I know that! That's why I'm working on the Sitting Bull gags.

CAPTAIN

Sitting Bull gags?

CUSTER

Naturally. I always have my writers prepare me special material for any new engagement. It keeps my patter nice and fresh.

CAPTAIN

But ... how can you do such a thing?

CUSTER

Simple. I have Buzz and Dwight here write it all up on cue-cards, then they crouch down behind a rock so the redskins can't see I'm reading it. Never fails.

CAPTAIN

General Custer, I don't think you see the point at all. Here we are, outnumbered 500 to one, about to be bloodily slaughtered, and you're writing Sitting Bull gags! It's time we faced facts, sir - this particular method of defence just isn't working. Look at the records. (HE UNROLLS A UNITED STATES GOVERNMENT DOCUMENT) Five thousand men massacred at Wounded Knee when General Levine read out comic newsflashes to the Blackfeet. 42,000 men sliced to pieces when General Munroe went into his drunk-trying-to-find-the-keyhole routine before fifty thousand scalp-hungry Comanches at Twisted Buttock Pass. 47,000 given the tomahawk treatment when General McKinley's troops did Max Wall walks to the massed tribes of the Shawnee at Mangled Pancreas Gulch. I mean, ask yourself, General ... how many U.S. soldiers have been killed in these wars so far?

CUSTER

Well ... six hundred and eighty thousand.

CAPTAIN

And how many Indians have been killed in retaliation?

CUSTER

Er ... approximately .. one thousand and fifty.

CAPTAIN

And how many exactly?

CUSTER

Four.

CAPTAIN

Four. And three of those got killed doing the "menacing appearance over the hill" bit near an unexpectedly sharp cliff.

CUSTER

Well what do you suggest we do then?

CAPTAIN

Well my idea is this. Don't use up all your topical material by blowing it in the first half, but try to hold back a few real woofers for the one-liner spot at the end.

SCENE NINE:- THE BATTLE OF THE LITTLE BIGHORN. BODIES EVERYWHERE. THE SAND IS CAKED WITH BLOOD. PEOPLE STAGGERING BACK AND FORTH WITH SWORDS THROUGH THEIR SIDES TO GIVE THE IMPRESSION OF CARNAGE. SHOTS OF SOLDIERS WRITING TO H.Q. FOR A TRANSFER. GENERAL SWIRL OF DUST, COMMOTION AND FLESH BEING CARVED UP.

CUSTER IS STANDING ON A SMALL PLATFORM IN THE MIDDLE, HOLDING A VIOLIN. UNSEEN BY THE MARAUDING INDIANS, TWO CAVALRYMEN ARE CROUCHED UNDERNEATH A SMALL ROCK, HOLDING UP GIANT CUE-CARDS TO GIVE THE IMPRESSION IT IS ALL AD LIB.

CUSTER

You know it's something of an honour to be here tonight. I don't get to go to too many bloody slaughters these days. I figure that watching <u>one</u> Yankees away game a season is quite enough.

(THE INDIANS LAUGH)

CUSTER

Say, I haven't seen this many knives in the back since the Nixon Administration was in office.

(THE INDIANS LAUGH)

CUSTER

It's true, you know if white man speak with forked tongue, Tricky Dicky musta had a canteen o'cutlery in there.

(THE INDIANS LAUGH)

CUSTER

Well it's been tremendous being here, and all I'd like to say in conclusion is...

(A SMALL FIVE-PIECE ORCHESTRA ON A LEDGE ABOVE STRIKE UP "THANKS FOR THE MEMORY")

CUSTER

Thanks for the memory
Your braves have gone and scalped me
Now I feel a proper mug.
I never knew Sinatra was
So desperate for a rug
Oh thank you so much.

Thanks for the memory
You've cut off all my arms and legs
And left me here for dead.
I guess you musta liked me
Or you'd soon cut off my --- WURGHHHH!!

(THE INDIANS LAUGH)

Metro-Golda-Meir
Burbank, Hollywood
USA, Shepperton

6.13.51.

Sir,
This screenplay contains wit, charm, sophistication,
and three other words we couldn't understand as well.
No can do at the moment, I'm afraid, we're up to here
with the new space-sex movie "Oh Black Hole of
Calcutta", starring Indira Ghandi's mouth. Sorry can't
be of more help on this one, but I'm sure you know the
difficult position. The right leg is first placed on
the floor resting against the left buttock. This then
...towards the lady's thighs so that one can
...gradually. It is strictly legal but
...places where a lot of
...decency.

July 52

18 SUNDAY *April Fool's day*

Wife settled bill with milkman this morning then got up. Still not much luck with my writing...
Part-time job yesterday on a farm, cleaning out the pigs, but couldn't get my arm out afterwards... Haaaaaaa. Got that one from a cracker. Didn't catch her name.
6pm. Dashed off specimin material for great new explorer-type book, - will send to publishers tomorrow...

No.

OFFICE STAMP

POST OFFICE

TELEGRAM

Charges to pay

Tariff £
V.A.T. £
Total £

Prefix. Time handed in. Office of origin and Service Instructions. Words.

+PR2 8.45 LONDON X50

At
To
By

RECEIVED
From
By

ALLENANDUNWIN BOOKS BRIT MUSEUM 1895 WC1 =
ENCLOSE WITH TELEGRAM FANTASTIC NEW BOOK
BY HEYADALI JUST FINISHED TODAY STOP NEW
GIRLFRIEND AMAZINGLY HEALTHY TEETH YOU KNOW
DRAWER SEVENTEEN CATDISTMORT +

For free repetition of doubtful words telephone "TELEGRAMS ENQUIRY" or call, with this form at office of delivery. Other enquiries should be accompanied by this form, and, if possible, the envelope.

(181455) Dd. 363162 9/75 Hw.

Charges to pay

Tariff £
V.A.T. £
Total £

RECEIVED
From
By

POST OFFICE
TELEGRAM

Prefix. Time handed in. Office of origin and Service Instructions. Words.

No.
OFFICE STAMP

S2304 8.50 LONDON X51

At m
To
By

CROYDON ST1 FF5 =

QUERY LAST ITEM = UNWINANDALLEN+

(181455) Dd. 363162 9/75 Hw.

For free rep...

Charges to pay

Tariff £
V.A.T. £
Total £

RECEIVED
From
By

POST OFFICE
TELEGRAM

Prefix. Time handed in. Office of origin and Service Instructions. Words.

No.
OFFICE STAMP

At m
To
By

SEX + 69 8.51 LONDON

ALIENANDUNWIN BOOKS BRIT EKLAND MUSEUM
STREET = AFFIRMATION STOP KEEPS IN GLASS
LUCOZADE OVERNIGHT STOP HAAAA STOP
CONTINUES EDIT STOP GET THESE BACK
LORRIES STOP CROYDON +

For free repetiti... or call, with this form at office of delivery. Other enquiries should be accompanied by this form, and, if possible, the envelope.

(181455) Dd. 363162 9/75 Hw.

DAY ONE. Roaldali sails to South America in craft made entirely from egg boxes, sellotape and washing-up liquid bottles. Mission: to prove the Ancient Aztecs watched Blue Peter . . .

THE VOYAGE OF SALVADOR ROALDALI

DAY TWO. Expedition begins.

July 18th — with just a handful of bosoms and only enough provisions to last until they run out, we set out on the first leg of our donkey. Now, at long last we are to upend the classical bourgeois theories of ironing! Our journey starts here, at Paramaribo, making for the southern jungles of Valparaiso in Chile!

Oct. 14th — discovered this morning that I have a hole in my sleeping bag. This would explain why I have been losing so much sleep. The heat is becoming unbearable, so I have been forced to stop setting fire to my beard. These conditions confirm my worst fears... we are now dangerously low on jokes.

DAY 91. THE HEAT GROWS STEADILY MORE OPPRESSIVE. ROALDALI TELLS HIS MEN TO STICK TOGETHER. ONE OF THEM SAYS HE HAS BEEN DOING THIS FOR THE LAST WEEK . . . THUS USING UP THEIR LAST GAG . . .

BUT THE JOURNEY WAS NOT TO BE AN EASY ONE.

July 31st — Thirteen days later and we have still got only as far as here... about 12 m.m. away on a map of South America. We decide to travel across the real S. America instead.

IN ORDER TO REACH THE LOWER ANDES, ROALDALI HAD CHOSEN TO TAKE THE MOST EVIL AND TREACHEROUS ROUTE OF ALL – THE SO-CALLED "PRETTY WAY"! WITHIN HOURS HE WAS STRICKEN BY THE MOST HIDEOUS HORROR KNOWN TO ECCENTRIC EXPLORERS: "MAL DE PANTALON" . . . UNDERPANTS SICKNESS!

August 2nd. Deprived of my natural environment of lurching about in a tiny boat wearing nothing but a pair of revolting goatskin shorts was more than I could bear. We are told the nauseous effects of cool, clean, cotton-and-polyester Y-fronts is something one grows used to in time... for my own part I can think of no worse foreign body to have next to my skin. (Except for Greta-von Spuntumbag of Goering-on-sea.

November 1st — More trouble with the llamas. During the night they formed a workers co-operative with mandatory full-committee approval of all operational decisions and ratification rights on all packloads they are asked to carry. I shoot them.

DAY 106. THE PICTURE BECOMES EVER BLEAKER. THE MORALE OF THE MEN IS AT ITS LOWEST EBB SINCE CAPTAIN FITZSMOTH CAME ACROSS TEN STARK NAKED, EROTICALLY POSED GIRLS UNDER A PALM TREE, AND THEN FOUND OUT HE WAS A MIRAGE.

BUT ONLY THREE DAYS LATER, TRAGEDY STRIKES. MEN ARE GOING DOWN LIKE FLIES: SLOWLY AND VERY CAREFULLY. WATER RATIONS ARE SO LOW THEY HAVE TO START DILUTING IT. FORTUNATELY, THEY ARE STILL WELL STOCKED UP ON LUNCHEON VOUCHERS, BUT, WITH THE PARTY NOW HEAVILY DEPLETED, ROALDALI IS FORCED TO REORGANISE HIS WORKFORCE: THE 58,000 MEN WITH BIG PENCILS DRAWING LINES IN THE SEA AROUND THE COAST ARE RECALLED, AND THEY DECIDE TO RISK THE REST OF THE JOURNEY WITH ONLY A SINGLE PEN-AND-INK OUTLINE . . .

December 8th — My biographer was bitten during the night by a snake, but says it is not serious — the snake was merely a one-night stand. However, he decides to give up further documentary on the expedition — leaving me to explain it for myself.

PANDES

ANDES

PRETTY WAY

WET BITS

TEDDES

Valparaiso

SEE OPPOSITE

MYSTERIES OF THE AGE

by Salvador Z. Roaldali

A few years ago now I postulated my theory that the Earth was in actual fact a Maltezer. Sceptics derided this credo on the grounds that there is an apparent size discrepancy: The Earth has a diameter of some 12,756 miles, the average Maltezer – taking into account regional fluctuations – approximately five-eighths of an inch. This, the so-called "Maltezer Paradox", is but one of the great mysteries of our Age. My trip to Chile will demonstrate another.

Evidence I have compiled over past months shows what I have suspected for many years: that the empires of the Ancient World were founded, not by the Mayans or the Incas or the Phoenicians, but by a housewife from Crawley. This is the corollary of my theory that the early civilisations shared a culture based on crisply laundered ironing.

Research demonstrates that the ancient Egyptians, for instance, possessed a Hoover steam-spray with adjustable thermostatic controls far superior to anything we know today. People dispute this, but have you seen the *creases* in those Pyramids? They weren't sent to Sketchley, you know! No, the Egyptians used enormous ramps, and teams of thousands of slaves would haul the giant irons up the sides . . .

In the Spring of 1979 I spent six months ascending the Giant Ziggurat of Mesopotamia for one reason only: to find a nozzle; to prove that this was no temple at all, but a huge aerosol can of Robin Spray Starch. In August I struck it rich: I found *no nozzle!!* You know how those nozzles are always coming off? Everything fitted perfectly!

And so to my expedition into the Lower Andes. After a somewhat shaky start, eventually my dedication began to bear fruit. Noticing that the South American Pampas were the flattest plains in Peru, I was convinced that here was the Ironing Board of the World! Then, a month later, whilst seeking the candy-striped stretch-cover inside the Amazon Basin – a breakthrough! We stumbled across an old dying native. He claimed to be the very man who used to flick water over the Russian Steppes so the wrinkles could be removed without scorching.

There was now but one course open to us: rush back home to Britain and write the best-selling adventure story for the Christmas market without delay! And here we are . . .

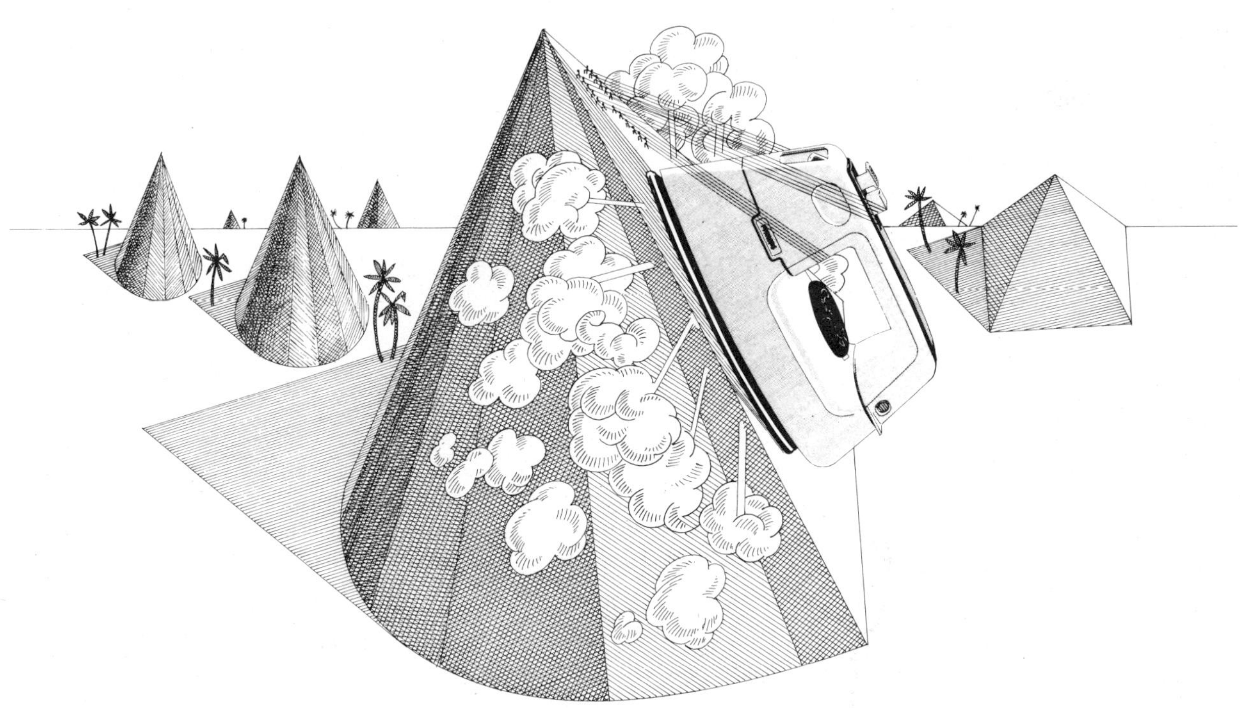

RIDDLE OF THE PYRAMIDS

Why has the 'marble funeral monolith' setting been removed from modern irons? Is the blank space between 'Acrilan' and 'Silk/Rayon' anything to do with this?

C.F. O'Schwartz's

EAT SOL'S PIES

1955

EBRUARY

14 SUN *Massacring Sunday*

Dog missing. Got him wider lamp-post. Started new book on life and times of escapologist Harry Houdini, following discovery in attic of old posters and cuttings...

342 Canal St., Cincinnati PRESENTS

WEEK OF NOVEMBER 1st 1934

ELMA BRAATZ

SEE THEM WOBBLE" in her SENSATIONAL REVUE OF '38D: ... "THANKS FOR THE MAMMARY" "There'll be black eyes in the front row tonight, Bub!"

AND FULL SUPPORTING GARMENTS

ERNESTINE BLATSTEIN

presents
"PANCREAS TIME"
Assisted by Gwendolyn Carp

SADIE BRAKAAKQRZTZKY

A SMILE, A SONG & A BLOOD SAMPLE

A few minutes with

FIFI BALBINSTEIN

Followed by a few questions from

Lt. O'REILLY OF THE VICE SQUAD

"Book Him, Danno!"

WALT "TWO NAVELS" BRICUSSE

NOVELTY IMPRESSIONS OF JIMMY DURANTE

CHAS. NATKE
and his ointment

ESTELLE Q. FLAGG

"MIND MY THEOREM!" Mime Artiste with no difference

THE ~~TWELVE~~ TWENTY FOUR FLYING KARENSKYS

Something new upon the high wire
"INCISIVE" — The Cheese Cutter's Chronicle

J. EDGAR HOOVER AND CO.

"Get a load of those Gams"

SHORT BUT SWEET

TRISTRAN "FLASHER" LE VERE

presents: "WANT SOME NICE CANDY, SONNY?"
"Gives a whole new meaning to Mackintoshes Rollo"
— *The Ni*

Out on Parole

"HOT LIPS" DEVINE & WILBUR

(THE HUMAN LOI
"There She Blows!"

KLEIN'S NEMATODES

IN A PROGRAM OF PARASITIC JINKS

LEIBNIZ (1646-1716)

"Dead but Mathematical"

LANA LUGG with

DUNCAN THE TALKING TIBETAN O

present:
"YAKKETY YAK"

(THERE WILL BE AN INTERVAL OF 20 MINS)

HARRY HOUDINI
SOME FAINTLY INTERESTING THINGS

EARS PIERCED!
HAIR REMOVED!
TEETH STRAIGHTENED!

by: L. Scarlotti and his boys, 692 E.49th, Nixon, Oregon.

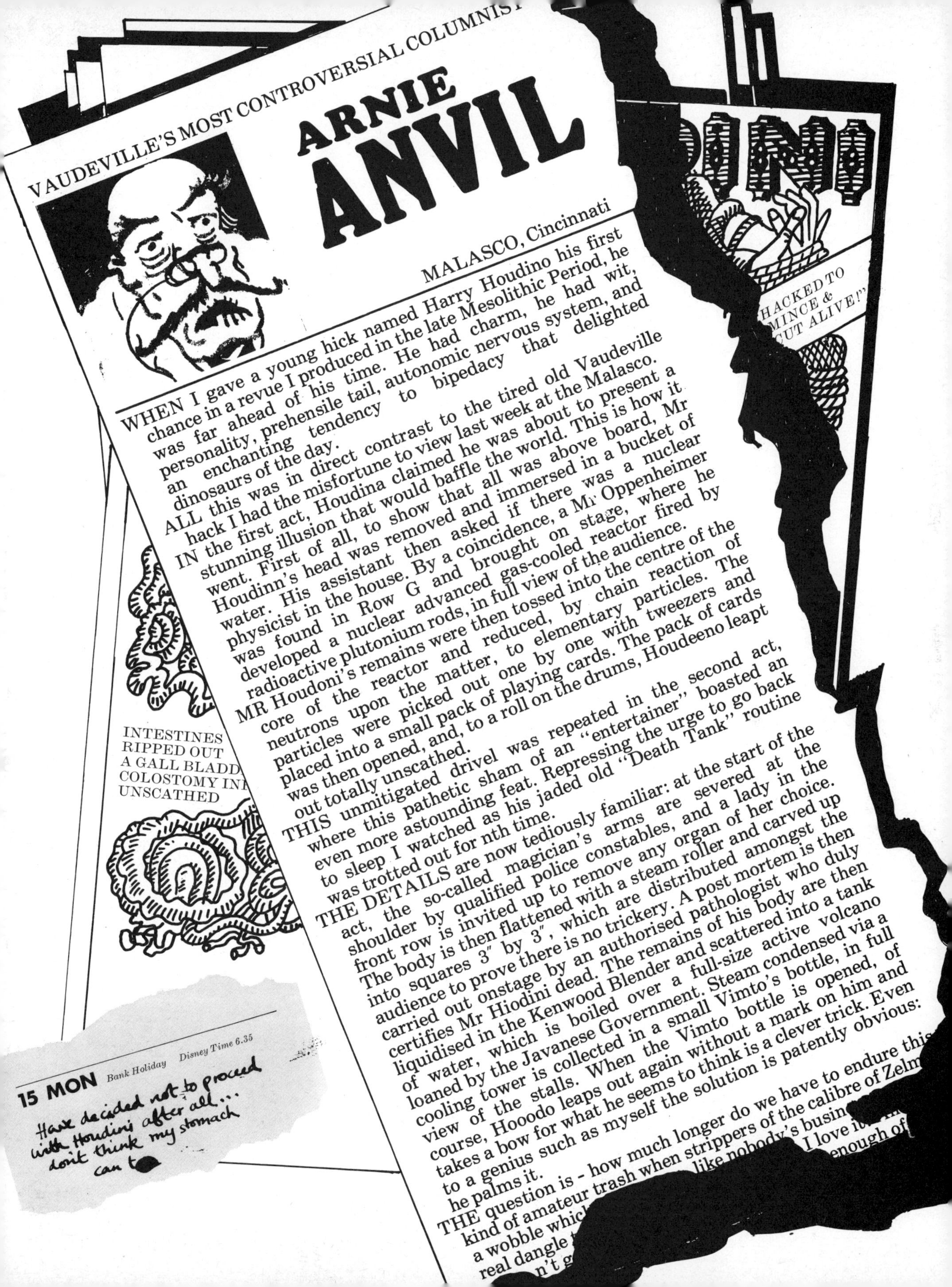

VAUDEVILLE'S MOST CONTROVERSIAL COLUMNIST

ARNIE ANVIL

MALASCO, Cincinnati

WHEN I gave a young hick named Harry Houdino his first chance in a revue I produced in the late Mesolithic Period, he was far ahead of his time. He had charm, he had wit, personality, prehensile tail, autonomic nervous system, and an enchanting tendency to bipedacy that delighted dinosaurs of the day.

ALL this was in direct contrast to the tired old Vaudeville hack I had the misfortune to view last week at the Malasco.

IN the first act, Houdina claimed he was about to present a stunning illusion that would baffle the world. This is how it went. First of all, to show that all was above board, Mr Houdinn's head was removed and immersed in a bucket of water. His assistant then asked if there was a nuclear physicist in the house. By a coincidence, a Mr Oppenheimer was found in Row G and brought on stage, where he developed a nuclear advanced gas-cooled reactor fired by radioactive plutonium rods, in full view of the audience. MR Houdoni's remains were then tossed into the centre of the core of the reactor and reduced, by chain reaction of neutrons upon the matter, to elementary particles. The particles were picked out one by one with tweezers and placed into a small pack of playing cards. The pack of cards was then opened, and, to a roll on the drums, Houdeeno leapt out totally unscathed.

THIS unmitigated drivel was repeated in the second act, where this pathetic sham of an "entertainer" boasted an even more astounding feat. Repressing the urge to go back to sleep I watched as his jaded old "Death Tank" routine was trotted out for nth time.

THE DETAILS are now tediously familiar: at the start of the act, the so-called magician's arms are severed at the shoulder by qualified police constables, and a lady in the front row is invited up to remove any organ of her choice. The body is then flattened with a steam roller and carved up into squares 3″ by 3″, which are distributed amongst the audience to prove there is no trickery. A post mortem is then carried out onstage by an authorised pathologist who duly certifies Mr Hiodini dead. The remains of his body are then liquidised in the Kenwood Blender and scattered into a tank of water, which is boiled over a full-size active volcano loaned by the Javanese Government. Steam condensed via a cooling tower is collected in a small Vimto bottle, in full view of the stalls. When the Vimto bottle is opened, of course, Hooodo leaps out again without a mark on him and takes a bow for what he seems to think is a clever trick. Even to a genius such as myself the solution is patently obvious: he palms it.

THE question is - how much longer do we have to endure this kind of amateur trash when strippers of the calibre of Zelm… a wobble which… like nobody's busin… I love it… enough of… real dangle… n't g…

23 WED Freezing cold today. Passed several icicles on way to work. V. painful. Sent publishers sample stuff for new medical book...

The Body in Question

by A Doctor

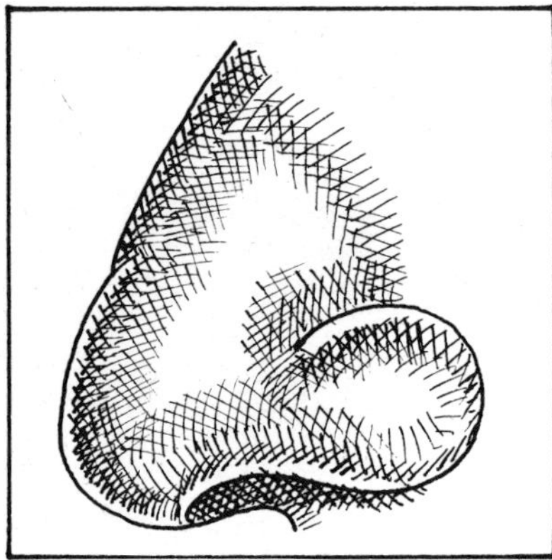

The author (detail).

The human body is truly the most remarkable object Nature has ever devised. We can touch it, feel it, pinch it, squeeze it, and generally get arrested for it. Like it or not, it has become part of our daily lives, and people who have had their bodies removed in operations find rehabilitation no easy matter.

Why should this be? Well, personally I have always found the easiest way to answer this question is to crouch about on the seashore wearing baggy corduroy trousers, while jerking my arms up and down like an octopus with St Vitus's Dance. And I think there is probably a lot of truth in this.

Medicine in Britain today is, thankfully, an advanced and highly efficient affair. Under the National Health Service, if a patient needs treating badly he will be admitted to hospital, and treated badly straight away. Just over a century ago, however, this was not the case. Knowledge of medical science was, at its best, non-existent. Doctors tended to fall into two main categories: Body Specialists, i.e. those who dealt with the pink thing underneath the clothes; and Lemon Specialists: those specialising in diseases of the human lemon. Rudimentary tuition was normally carried out at St Tesco's Medical College, where most of the professors were on special offer because they were a bit dented. One such eminent physician of the day was Horace Loony.

Loony is generally credited as being the first medic to observe a link in the treatments of smallpox and its less virulent strain, cowpox, which affected only cows. A mild infection of the latter, he reasoned, could act as resistance against the former. The treatment became obvious in a blinding flash. Taking a

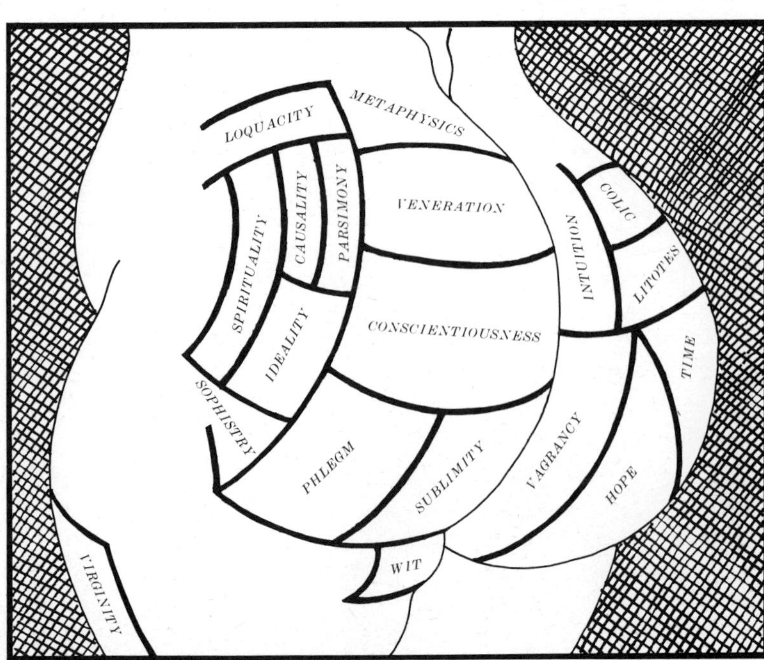

The 16th-century science of Posteriorology held that different areas of the human bottom were responsible for the different faculties of Man. So-called posteriorologists would spend hours on end inspecting a bottom, for a fee of between 20 and 30 guineas – depending on how much the patient charged.

small boy who had gone down with smallpox, Loony proceeded to inject 5,000 litres of cow into his bloodstream. The effect was dramatic: in just six hours Loony had been trussed up in a strait jacket and carted off in a little yellow van.

But if medical treatments then were crude, the illnesses were even more so. That's to say, it wasn't until great visionaries like Sir Joseph Typhus and Dr William Bubo came along that the development of serious disorders began to show real promise.

For Typhus progress, though slow, was steady. In 1796 he began in a small way by stumbling across a rare disease of the left sock. Two years later he perfected a virus which was fatal to woodworms but left the heads of professional boxers intact. And by 1805 we see from his notes that Typhus felt close to success:

> 'That I have now developed the nasty disease I have been searching for all these years I am convinced. My one problem remains how best to spread it. My initial method of advertising it in a newsagent's window – 'plague available, easy terms' – seems to have drawn little response. However, I am now certain that the plague may in fact be spread by *rats*. All it requires is one simple bite to transfer it to the human body.'

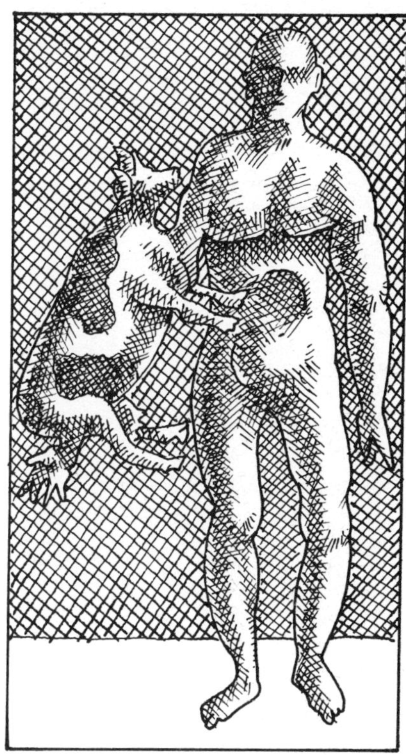

Early attempts to deal with Smallpox involved injecting a cow into the patient's bloodstream.

And so, for fourteen years, Typhus waited patiently for someone to go out and bite a rat. Without success. In fact, when Typhus finally unveiled his plans for a new plague to his colleagues at St Bart's Hospital for Frostbite and Other Rare Tropical Diseases, everyone in the audience just laughed at him. As a result, he toured with the speech around the clubs, and was eventually signed up for a spot on the Tom O'Connor Show, following his death in 1821.

By now Typhus and Bubo had opened up the floodgates. In the years that followed the perfection of new and more virulent complaints advanced by leaps and bounds, with the work of people like Louis Gangrene, Madame Scurvy, Sir Hubert Rickets, and Jan Van Der Shingles.

In Vienna, Professor Ernst Vertigo rise to dizzy heights, and of the researchers in Russia Leonid Bodyodour and Georgi Halitosis were acknowledged as being far and away the best.

In Rouen, however, two young French chemists, Armand and Gilbert Mump, were still struggling to find an effective disease of the neck. And in 1843 the Mump brothers were certain they had made the final breakthrough: during a routine examination of King Phillipe one afternoon they pointed out a slight swelling under his left ear. The King dismissed the idea, saying the swelling was 'cobblers'. Unfortunately the reverse was also true. And he had very few children after that.

Surgeons in hospitals today are, of course, rather more advanced than their predecessors. That's to say, surgeons in hospitals today are rather more advanced than their predecessors – as we can see from the following extract from the BBC documentary programme 'Your Life in Their Hands' . . .

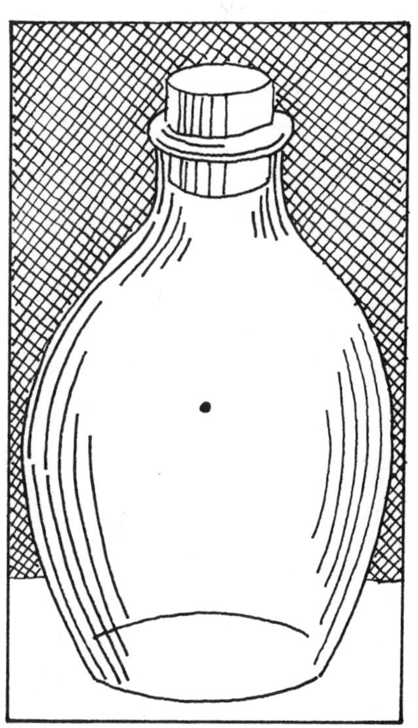

The prototype Measle, developed in 1831 by Garibaldi.

SCENE: STEPNEY ACCIDENT AND MATERNITY WING. DAY.

SISTER: Nurse. Go and treat that man in Bed Fourteen would you. It's his birthday.

NURSE: Very good, sister.

FLARK: Excuse me, sister, I wonder if you can help me.

SISTER: Plastic Surgery's down the corridor, sir.

FLARK: No, no – I've got a question to ask.

SISTER: Go right ahead, sir.

FLARK: You're very kind, but that wasn't the question. It's my wife. She was involved in two accidents this morning. She crashed her car into a brick wall, a concrete bollard, and John Travolta.

SISTER: That's *three* accidents, sir.

FLARK: No, only two *accidents*. But is it possible for me to see how's she's getting on?

SISTER: You'll want Dr Thrimpson. He's dealing with all Casualty ops today. Through here.

FLARK: Thank you.

HE ENTERS A SMALL OFFICE WITH PICTURES OF PAGE THREE GIRLS ALL OVER THE WALLS. A TRANSISTOR RADIO IS BLARING OUT A BEE GEES RECORD. DR THRIMPSON IS SITTING WITH HIS FEET UP ON THE DESK CHECKING OFF HORSES IN THE RACING COLUMN.

FLARK: Good morning, doctor. My name's Flark, my wife was admitted this morning with very heavy injuries. I wondered if you could help me . . . How is she?

DOCTOR: Well I don't know till I've checked, do I, Mahatma? What colour was she?

FLARK: I'm sorry?

DOCTOR: What colour?

FLARK: Er . . . well, sort of *flesh*-coloured, doctor.

DOCTOR: Hang about, Pope . . .
HE SLIDES OPEN A DOOR.

DOCTOR: Les! Have we had an off-pink female in – dented down the right-hand side?

LES: I'm doing it now!

HE SLIDES THE DOOR SHUT AGAIN.

DOCTOR: Won't keep you long, District Attorney. (SINGS:) Everybody loves somebody sometime . . .

FLARK: Just a minute – what were all those men in boiler suits doing in that operating theatre?

THE PHONE RINGS.

DOCTOR: Half a ticko, Dalai Lama. (ANSWERS IT) West Stepney General. What's that, you've just been run over by a steamroller, sir or madam? . . . Phoo . . . no, not before Christmas now, Sheriff . . . *What* blood group? "O"? Cor blimey, what's this – Old Tyme Music Hall? *No* chance, Dauphin! No . . . you can't get the corpuscles. (PUTS THE PHONE DOWN)

FLARK: Look, about my wife . . .

DOCTOR: Hang about, ref . . .
HE SLIDES OPEN THE DOOR AGAIN.

DOCTOR: Les! Is that old geezer's truss ready yet? I can't keep him hanging about much longer!
SLIDES IT SHUT AGAIN.

DOCTOR: Won't be long now, procurator fiscal.

FLARK: Look, I demand to see ——

THE PHONE RINGS AGAIN.

DOCTOR: One second *if* you please, Scipio . . . (ANSWERS IT) West Stepney General . . . Oh yeh, 1921 Grandmother, I remember. Be ready a week Wednesday, Master of Foxhounds . . . Yeh, well we had her up on the ramp, you know, and it was basically a fault in your overhead cranium, mounted on dodgy atlas and axis neck joints. That's it, Sabbatical Dean of

Humanities, so we put a new head on for you. No, no, it looks fine! We had a spare left over from a London bus conductor. Quick respray and it fitted a treat. OK? Bye for now then, Moderator of the Free Church of Scotland – bye. (PUTS PHONE DOWN. SINGS:) I left my heart in San Francisco . . .

FLARK: I've had a gutful of this . . .

DOCTOR: You're not the only one, Acting Ambassador Extraordinary and Plenipotentiary with the Italian Consulate in the province of Manitoba, I'm getting pretty pissed off with it myself.

GEORGE ALLEN & UNWIN

Dear Mr Croydon,

"The Body in Question"

The above manuscript was without question the most risibly atrocious apology for a textbook of modern medicine it has ever been our misfortune to peruse. Not only did it plumb the depths of incompetent, grossly misrepresented trash in a manner never before countenanced, it evinced reactions of physical nausea among those of our staff ill-omened to read it. Three were violently sick, six suffered spontaneous haemorrhaging and one took his own life rather than finish it to the end. It was, in short, the most despicably dreadful, nasty, horrid, evil, obnoxious, abject, odious and unpleasant, cankerous pile of ordure that has ever been my misfortune to experience. The excremental nature of your work leads me to warn you never to ever darken our doorsteps or any other place with your loathsome presen

Some ball points and she gave me.

28 MON Bank Holiday Disney Time 6.16

Letter back today from publishers re: Body In Question. They didn't say whether they're going to buy it or not... Not to worry, Am already just finishing off first detective novel! At last I'm sure I have come up with a winner...

Sir Waterbuffalo & Knighthood Limited
Lord Publishing House
Dame Fetter Lane
LONDON W1L 5ON

August 3rd 1956, O.B.E.

Eric Pode of Croydon Esq.,
Drawer Seventeen,
Catford & Dist. Mortuary,
Stepney ST1 FF5.

Dear Mr District Mortuary,

I note with interest your proposal for a new detective novel chronicling the adventures of a young American named Henry Baskerville, who falls heir to a British estate following the grizzly death of his Uncle Charles at the hands of a horrible spectral hound. This has an exciting ring about it and is sure to generate unbounded enthusiasm among all devotees of this genre of crime thriller. Unfortunately I have to tell you that it has already been done in 1902 by Sir Arthur Conan Doyle. I would therefore respectfully suggest that you bugger off out of it, you pimply little earwig's vomit, and stop wasting my time.

Yours extremely sincerely,

A man so rich it's unbelievable.

Drawer Seventeen
Catford & District Mortuary
Stepney
ST1 FF5

August 5th 1956.

Dear Sir Unbelievable,

Thank you for your letter. I am well thank you. I have just buggered off as requested and both of us feel much better for it. My dandruff has just been signed up for the title role in "White Christmas". Haaaaa. Got that one from not washing my hands properley. Hope you are well off.

Yours,

X

Eric Pode of Croydon
pp Eric Pode of Croydon.

(P.S. Here is the manuscript for "The Hound of the Baskervilles" as requested.)

I

LONDON was in the grip of a fog such as I had not witnessed in all my years of association with the great metropolis. Clouds of its foul vapour would curl through the cracks around the windows, and without the buildings and thoroughfares became so wreathed in the wretched stuff it was all a cab driver could do to see the bum of the horse in front of him. Never have I encountered such a treacherous species of smog, choking the capital and polluting the very nostrils of all whose singular misfortune it was to be out in those nightmare conditions.

A word of apology, incidentally, about the use of the word bum there.

Without question these were grim, gloomy times. For my own part I know that a sense of uneasy melancholy had replaced my normal sanguine disposition. There was certainly no offence intended. In using the word bum, I mean. Sorry to harp on about it, but I know there are some extremely bum-sensitive people about, and I wouldn't like them to think I was conducting some sort of personal vendetta against them by sticking the word bum under their noses just for the sake of it.

Affairs of State were entering a critical period both at home and abroad, and the political climate was tense. Gathering war-clouds in Europe seemed to presage desperate days ahead. On reflection, I suppose, a milder term like botty might have been a safer bet. Better than bum, anyway. Six bums on one page – seven including that one – really is a bit of a gaff. Still, no use grizzling about it now, the damage is done, that's the way of the world. Best to let sleeping bums lie, probably. In short, the national mood was one of sombre disquiet.

On a singularly chill November evening, when none but a madman would have ventured forth alone through those fog-filled London backstreets, my good friend Inspector Lestrade decided to venture forth alone through those fog-filled London backstreets, and found himself at length in that dingy quarter known as Soho. Here, it is said, the women are good for nothing, though in my experience they charge about twenty quid. Ignoring such enticements by means of a trouser pocket filled with cold water, Lestrade found his way towards a seedy little ale-house, where, doffing his front teeth to the bouncer on the door, he stepped inside.

Through the haze of smoke which filled the tavern he identified the landlord, a rather confused man with a bald tyre and a spare head.

"Good evening, I've come for a meal."

"If you have a word with the barmaid I'm sure she'll accommodate you on a table."

"Yes, she looks the type. But first I must eat. I'm to meet a Doctor James Mortimer here – in fact, I think I see him over in the corner."

That Mortimer was a stout man you could tell from the empty bottles in his beard. Yet his thickset appearance belied that inherent delicacy common to most members of the medical profession. This was confirmed by the manner in which he was carrying out an autopsy on the soup, and his dark bushy eyebrows twitched nervously, as if in love with something in the salad.

"So sorry I'm late, Mortimer." Lestrade scraped a chair across the floor and flopped wearily into it. His forehead wore a furrowed expression which he took off and laid in his lap. "I've been held up on these abominable Whitechapel murders. Baffling thing. I confess I'm as confused as a hedgehog in Reginald Bosanquet's dressing room."

"Confused?"

"What to call him, doctor – what to call him. We've had a number of suggested names, but somehow none of them feel quite right. Still, that's my worry, and not yours. Why did you ask me to meet you here?"

"Inspector Lestrade, I have a story to tell. A grim, blood-curdling story of . . . The Curse of the Baskervilles. Are you listening carefully?"

"Twenty to six."

"Then I'll begin."

The old West Country practitioner leaned forward and lowered his voice.

"As you may be aware, Inspector, not long ago I used to sit on a special medical board. But now I just use the ointment."

"I'd heard something to that effect."

"Well, a month ago I had occasion to call on a neighbour of mine, Sir Charles Baskerville. The journey across Dartmoor was, as always, a rough and uncomfortable one, and I felt a great sense of relief when I finally dismounted from my horse and climbed out of the carriage.

"At the door I was met by Sir Charles's butler, Barrymore . . ."

II

"Ah, Doctor Mortimer. The very man I wish to see."

"What is it, Barrymore?"

The old retainer shuffled uneasily forward.

"I seem to be having trouble with my artificial leg, doctor."

"I see."

"It's getting a bit, well, uncomfortable."

"Hmmmm . . ." Mortimer eyed his patient up and down. "All in all it's hardly surprising, is it?"

"How do you mean, doctor?"

"Well, an artificial leg *would* be a little on the awkward side when you've still got two perfectly good legs of your own."

The butler considered this.

"I've got a *boil* on the left one."

"I don't care. That hardly necessitates the fitting of an additional prosthetic limb, now does it?"

"Better to be safe than sorry. Anyway, it's not right. It's meant to be completely undetectable."

"I'm afraid the sheer numerical factor would tend to be a giveaway in that area, Mr Barrymore."

"Well that's no good – I don't want everyone knowing I wear an artificial leg."

"In that case why don't you wear it somewhere more sensible?"

"What do you mean?"

"It wasn't designed to go on your head."

"There you are you see! I never told you it was on my head!"

"Mr Barrymore, you have a three-foot-high top hat on."

"Ah."

"Now stop wasting my time and show me to the lift."

"We haven't got a lift in this building, sir."

"Yes you have – that little room over there that keeps going up and down."

"We've had a number of suggested names, but somehow none of them feel quite right . . ."

"That's the Honeymoon Suite, sir."

"In that case just show me to Sir Charles's study."

"Sir."

Down a long, musty corridor they walked for what seemed like ages but was in fact four and a half years. At length they joined the main arterial corridor for the library, where they forked left onto the central broom-cupboard bypass via the three-lane ring corridor. This took them onto the C1520 past the scullery-lounge intersection, taking the third exit at the multi-staircase flyover. On and on they travelled, until suddenly it occurred to Mortimer that they had gone horribly wrong: Baskerville Hall was in fact a little cottage with only four rooms. Realising this they reached the study in seconds.

And yet, when they entered the room, it was completely bare, save for one wall which was wearing underpants. Of Sir Charles there was no sign. On the table by the fire stood a glass of brandy. Only half of it had been drunk, and what was even stranger was that it was the bottom half. A book lay half-open on the seat of the chair, many of the words still unread. And in the ashtray Mortimer noticed not one, but two cigar-ends, joined together by a cigar.

Over in the doorway there was a door, which was half-open and half-Negro.

"Sir Charles – he's gone out on the moor . . ." Barrymore's face turned a deathly shade of white.

"Well, what of it? He probably fancied some fresh air."

"No sir, you don't understand. There's something out on that moor that . . ."

Hardly had Barrymore got the last three dots out of his mouth when something horrible happened. From outside, on those windswept deserted moorlands came the most hideous cry ever to pass the lips of mortal man. Then a monstrous, unearthly baying sound, followed by a noise of ripping flesh, and such ear-piercing agonised screams as would chill the blood of even the most hardened.

"My God! It's Sir Charles! He's . . . he's . . . he's just eaten a giant dog!"

"You're being silly again, Barrymore."

"Sorry."

III

"HMMM. A remarkable tale, Doctor Mortimer."

Lestrade stroked his chin thoughtfully and topped up the anti-freeze in his coffee as his companion concluded his narrative.

"Remarkable indeed, Inspector. When Sir Charles's body was found the next day at the foot of his leg rigor mortis had already set in and he had to be rushed straight away to the House of Lords. In fact he had been so badly mauled that the only way we could identify him was by his teeth, which fortunately were still in a glass of water by his bed."

"And who or what do you think was responsible for his death?"

"That is what I would like you to find out, Inspector. Sir Charles's nephew Henry moves into the hall tomorrow. He must be spared the same fate as his uncle."

"Fear not, Doctor Mortimer. I shall leave for Devon at once!"

In fact it was almost a quarter past once when the London detective finally set off for the sleepy backwater of Grimpen.

On his arrival he was met by the cosiest of pastoral scenes. Tangled gorse and carpets of moorland heather lay baking in the afternoon sun. Rabbits scampered playfully beneath their pie-crusts, and somewhere a duck gave itself a hernia trying to hatch a golf ball. Losing no time, Lestrade took over the library at Baskerville Hall and made it his centre of operations.

A week passed with little progress. But Lestrade's mind was active. Again and again he gazed at the portrait of old Sir Hugo Baskerville hanging over the fireplace, and couldn't help noticing how well the artist had caught the light on the noose. Yet still he could not fit the pieces together. Then, at noon on the Sunday, Dr Mortimer called round, hungry for news.

"This may be a shot in the dark, Mortimer, but it's my belief your friend was gored to death by some form of dog."

"Why so, Inspector?"

"The forensic boys scraped this off his left boot."

"My God. What on earth is it?"

"Eric Pode of Croydon.",

"Exactly. Now then, Mr Croydon, a few questions if you don't mind. And stick to the truth please, I'm not stupid, you know." Lestrade opened his pencil and licked his notebook.

"I gather you were one of Sir Charles's closest employees here."

"That's right, sir. Every day for the last 43 years I've had to spread manure on the vegetable patch."

"Oh? What did you grow?"

"Lonely."

"Hard life is it?"

"I got seven mouths to feed, sir."

"Really?"

"Yes, I cut myself shaving."

"Now I understand you were out on the moor that night."

"I'll never forget it, Mr Lestrade. I saw something that night that turned my hair completely white."

"What was it?"

"A flock of seagulls."

Hardly had Lestrade finished bludgeoning his interviewee about the head with the coal skuttle when the tall, gaunt figure of Sir Henry Baskerville appeared in the room, followed shortly afterwards by Sir Henry.

"Inspector, I am off now to Merripit House. The Stapletons have invited me to another of their fancy dress parties."

Doctor Mortimer's brow at once clouded over.

"Odd. Sir Charles was due to go to a fancy dress party on the night of his murder."

"Of course!" Lestrade slapped his forehead, punched his hand and sawed his leg off. "So that was why he was dressed up as a giant dog biscuit!"

"And here's Sir Henry going off to another one. Tell me, Henry, whose idea was it you should go as a six-foot-high can of Kennomeat?"

"Why, Stapleton's. Don't you think it suits me?"

"Mr Baskerville." Lestrade's voice was quiet but firm. "I must ask you not, under any circumstances, to venture out on your own on that moor tonight."

"Really, Inspector?"

"No. You must take this guard dog with you."

A horrible snarling sound was heard from the adjoining room. In an instant, Lestrade had stepped inside and emerged with an enormous beast whose red, glowing eyes seemed to beckon one into the very bowels of Hell itself.

"It . . . er . . . seems a little bit on the spectral side."

"Yes, you'll be all right with this police dog, sir. A man in a false beard sold it to me only this morning. Just what you need to protect you across those lonely moors."

"Oh. Righty-ho then." Sir Henry took the leash and made for the door. "We'll be off. Come on, Towser . . ." Having said which he opened the door and disappeared into the night.

From outside, on those windswept deserted moorlands came the most hideous cry ever to pass the lips of mortal man. Then a monstrous, unearthly baying sound, followed by a noise of ripping flesh, and such ear-piercing, agonised screams as would chill the blood of even the most hardened. Again.

Dr James Mortimer came away from the window and eyed his companion thoughtfully.

"Er . . . Inspector Lestrade."

"Yes?"

There was an uncomfortable pause.

"Never mind. It's just that . . . sometimes I can't help wondering whether I engaged the right detective on this case."

ARCHIE'S FISH 'N' CHIPS
REJECT

THE END

July 23

Dillinger's birthday:
■ Public holiday in Glasgow

Owing to B.B.C. cutbacks, was invited onto "Mastermind" programme!

BBC

MAGNUSSON: The next contender please. Your name please?

MAGNUSSON: Your occupation?

PODE: Eric Pode of Croydon.

MAGNUSSON: And your specialist subject?

PODE: I work for Lewisham Council as their chief accident black spot.

MAGNUSSON: And you have two minutes on "Answering One Question Behind Each Time", Mr Croydon, starting from ... Now. How long was Noah in the ark?

PODE: Answering one question behind each time.

MAGNUSSON: Correct. In G.P.O., what do the letters stand for?

PODE: Forty days and forty nights.

MAGNUSSON: Correct. What do the letters G.B. on a car mean?

PODE: General Post Office.

MAGNUSSON: Correct. What sort of boat is a junk?

PODE: It's made in Britain.

MAGNUSSON: Correct. What nationality was William the Conqueror?

PODE: Chinese with a flat bottom.

MAGNUSSON: Correct. Give me another name for the Playboy Club in Park Lane.

PODE: Norman.

MAGNUSSON: Correct. In 1956 what killed 40,000 rabbits?

PODE: The Bunny Club.

MAGNUSSON: Will you get the Hell out of here, you pimply-faced little dipstick ...

PODE: Myxomatosis.

15 WED

Entered my dog at Crufts. Got ten years.

MAY 1973

8 Sunday

Pancake Sunday in Cowes

Out on parole today … London is no longer the same place. Nor is London. Don't feel like work today, so have written to B.B.C. asking if I can be on their new "Superstars" programme …

BRITISH BROADCASTING CORPORATION
TELEVISION CENTRE WOOD LANE LONDON W12 7RJ
TELEPHONE 01-743 8000 TELEX: 265781
TELEGRAMS AND CABLES: TELECASTS LONDON TELEX

Eric Pode of Croydon Esq.
Drawer 17
Catford & Dist. Mortuary
Stepney ST1 FF5.

Dear Mrs 17

Thank you for your application to take part in our new series of "The Superstars" in your capacity as

East Ham Ear-cleaning-out Ace (Hankie-over-a-Hairpin Harriers)

Unfortunately we cannot offer you a place as:

- [ ] Your shoulders are not so wide you have to walk through doors sideways
- [ ] Your head is wider than your neck
- [ ] You do not sweat neatly in little bits up the middle of your vest
- [ ] Your stomach obscures your knees in a seated position
- [ ] Your speaking voice is not squeaky enough
- [x] You are a cadaverous little heap of snail's detritus
- [ ] Your name has fewer than 67 consonants in a row
- [ ] You are supposed to wear the jockstrap on the inside
- [ ] You can't come along just to do that in the showers

Thankyou once again for your interest, which is payable within 28 days, or illegal action will be taken.

Completely Empty

Head of Sports

CRYSTAL PALACE
NATIONAL FLESH-FLAUNTING CENTRE

THE INTERNATIONAL

SUPERSTARS

KIDNEY STONES SOMETIMES PASS OUT ON THEIR OWN . . .

SOUVENIR POGRUM

KROEF OELZE: Celebrated Dutch marathon cyclist and current holder of the sore parts of his bottom. Born: Rotterdam.

POKK-KOKKOLA YAAMIKI HAAMENGRÜND: Rumanian tug-of-war team. Said to be world's most athletic lover. Currently married to a trampoline.

OSS VØØTZGENHØØG: Bobsleigh supremo from Bruges. Wrestles bulldozers and cracks nuts by coughing very loudly. Born: Mt Olympus.

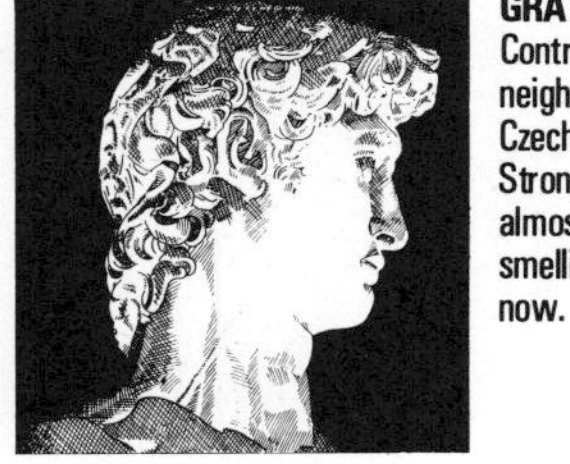

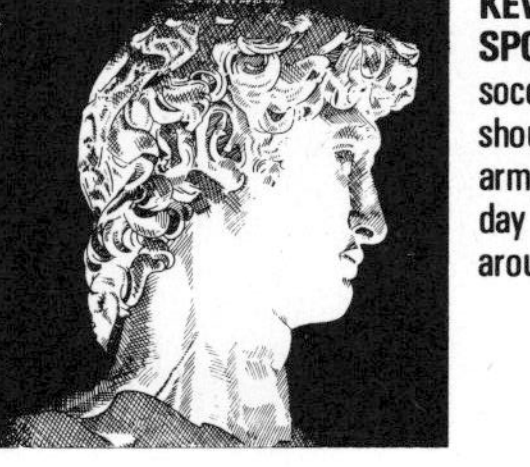

GRATZ TURDA: Controversial beggar-my-neighbour prodigy from Czechoslovakia in Poland. Strong as an ox and almost half as nice-smelling. Born: any day now.

GROK VOLGODONSK: Crack skittles ace from Finland. Vital statistics 23-stone-18-stone-36-stone. Does press-ups by lying on his back and pushing the world up and down. Born: Acme Pile-Driver Company.

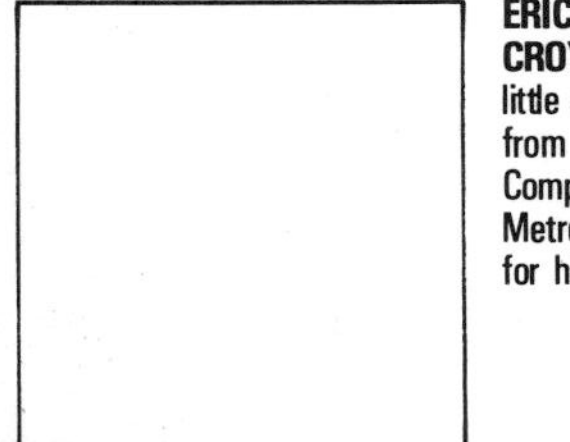

KEVIN IF-IT-MOVES-SPONSOR-IT: British soccer nonpareil, head and shoulders above his armpits. Exercises every day by jogging 25 miles around his bank balance.

GLADBACH WORMS: Westphalian fag-cards champ. Built like a tank and has tendency to go septic if left for too long. Born: A woman.

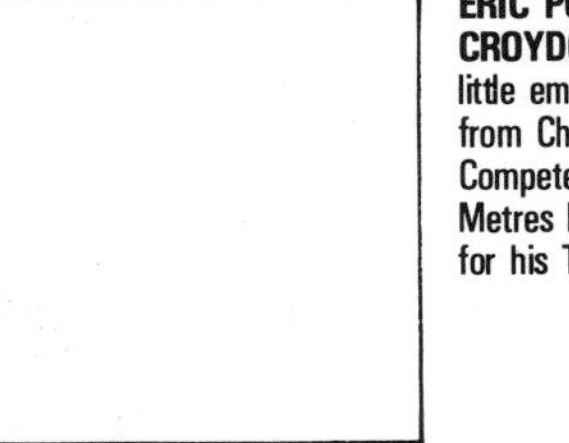

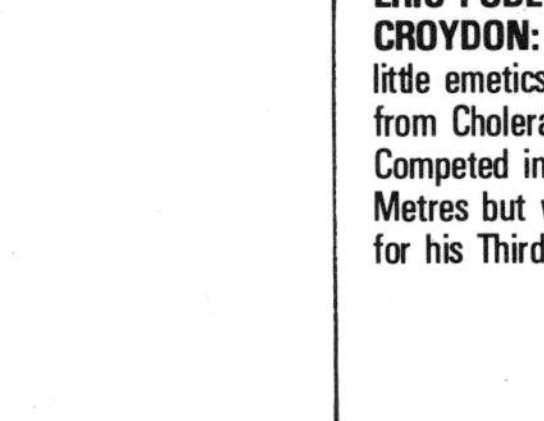

ERIC PODE OF CROYDON: Crack mucky little emetics supremo from Cholera in Surrey. Competed in Women's 100 Metres but was disqualified for his Third Leg.

THEY'RE BACK!

Once again, butch men from all over their girl friends are back at Crystal Palace thrusting their huge bronze muscles under our noses, and making weedy specimens like you and me feel life isn't worth living. The standards are, as always, high. Only yesterday, celebrated Squash Ace Mel Paparelli, 36-stone in stockinged legs and a former Mount Rushmore, was forced to take a sex-test, and failed on the emergency stop. His place is taken by our own Brian Haemorrhage, the celebrated boxing ace and roughage fan from Weybridge in deepest jockstraps.

Haemorrhage, a self-taught masochist and author of the best-selling book "Diana Dors the Hard Way", keeps himself in regular agonising pain by barbecuing his stomach on a small spit-roast. Today he will be attempting to shatter his own unrivalled record for viciously whipping yourself across the back with a length of copper wire: 8,964 lashes, which he set up last year in Helsinki, shortly before being admitted to the local mortuary for observation. So how confident is this brawny endo-skeletal plantigrade? I spoke to him today in the oven as he was plugging his ears with cotton wool to stop his brain falling out. "Om very confident on the squat-thrusts and the ankle-cracks, David. And Om very confident on the elbow-severs. I done 476 of them yesterday – one for each elbow." And how was the *counting* coming along? "Very good, David. I can count up to 384 now. From 383. So Om very confident on the neck fractures, and Om getting better all the time on the goolie-wrenches." But why does he do it? Why *does* he ceaselessly subject his body to this barbaric punishment? What possible point is there in this relentless inhuman self-mutilation day after day? This was the question Haemorrhage put to me, but I'm afraid I couldn't answer it. — D.V.

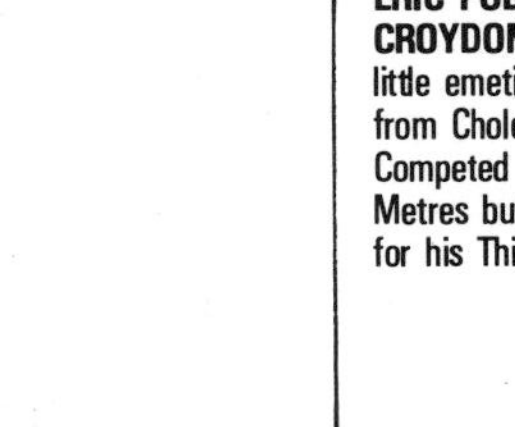

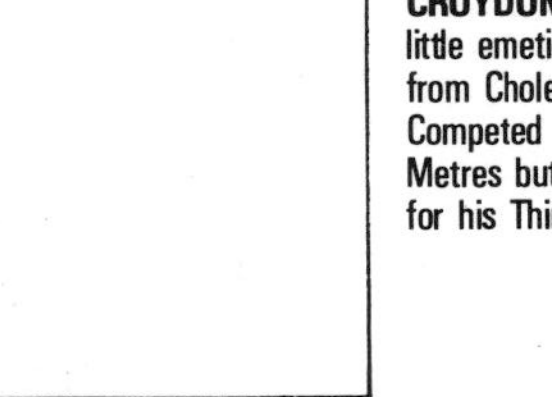

Britain's 25-year-old Brian Haemorrhage mincing himself up in training this week.

The Years

1974-1977

In April 1974 Croydon suffered from severe fits of violent coughing and had to undergo an emergency operation to remove his tonsils from the coal skuttle. For months he didn't have two ha'pennies to rub together, and had to use one ha'penny and a button. In his writings at this time he became heavily influenced by the works of Johnny Kwango and Honey Boy Zimba, the then all-in wrestlers . . . producing in June 1975 the "fixed" version of Keats's "Ode to Melancholy". During the summer he sojourned with Diana Ross and Harry Carpenter at their home in Florida, and took time off to promote his Alcatraz Outward Bound Scheme before moving on finally to the Mount Palomar Observatory in California to see Sir Frederick Hoyle, who was in Tokyo. In 1976 Croydon moved on to plays, drawing heavily for his inspiration from Harold Pinter, who had once said Good Morning to him from May 1938 to August 1941. Among his most famous oeuvres of this time: "Dredge of Crust", "The Pinking Wolf Semblances", "A Priest Gauge for Derry" and "Tryst Sustammerer Part Three". A brief period ensued during which he actually appeared onstage. In January of 1977 he opened in the West End and got six months. Later on he had a key part in The Mousetrap and the doctors had to use pliers. But probably the greatest single digression from his natural style was his tangental foray into the world of the comic strip. Not a single one of his efforts in this direction was ever published. Especially this one . . .

STORY... HAL SCHWARTE + GARDNER ZOZNSKIJ
INKS... GIL LEIPZIG + JMZKJL F. JSKZL JR.
ERIC PODE OF CROYDON REALLY
THE LEAGUE OF...
SUPER HEROES
The Roll Call
INVISIBLE KID
CAPTAIN ATOM
BOSOMS LASS
GREEN AEROSOL
BROBDINGNAG BOY
WHAT COULD IT MEAN? OUR GALLANT GANG OF CRUSADING CRIMEBUSTERS DOOMED???
HORRORS! WHAT GHASTLY GRIM GAM LURKED AT THE HEART OF THE TERROR THAT PUMMELLED AND PULVERISED OUR PRECIOUS PALS TO A PRETZEL?
READ ON ONLY IF YOU DARE, AS ONCE AGAIN OUR LOYAL LEGION OF LAW LORDS COME TO GRIPS WITH THE DEADLY
"MENACE of THE SLANTY BLOCK CAPITALS!!!"
CHOKE! GREEN DEATHONITE! I'M CHOKE! DYING! LUCKY FOR ME THIS SPLASH PANEL HAS NOTHING TO DO WITH THE REST OF THE STORY AS USUAL! CHOKE!!
CHOKE
CHOKE
ZZZT
ZZZT
ZZZT

T THE CITADEL OF SOMETHING BEGINNING
VITH "C", TOP SECRET ABODE OF THE LEAGUE
F SUPER-HEROES, A VITAL MEETING IS IN
PROGRESS...
SUPER
EROES
LEAGUE OF SU
THIS WA

WELL I THINK IT'S FAIR TO SAY THE APPLICATIONS FOR NEW MEMBERS HAVE BEEN PRETTY DISAPPOINTING!
CHECK! HOW COULD WE EVER TAKE ON SUPER HEROES LIKE THESE...
INVISIBLE KID
BOSOMS LASS

PICKO LAD! ...CAN PICK HIS NOSE AT WILL!...
...COMMANDER HORLICKS! CAN MAKE HOT MALTED-MILK BEDTIME DRINKS AT WILL!...

J'ONN J'ONZZ... TWIG SNIFFER FROM MARS, CAN SNIFF ALMOST ANY TWIG AT WILL...
...AND LASERMAN! SPELT LIKETHAT TO DISGUISE WHAT HE ACTUALLY DOES ON FRIDAY NIGHTS...
WELL, THERE'S STILL ONE FINAL APPLICANT—WE WE MAY AS WELL SEE HIM.
GREEN AEROSOL
RIGHT
BROBDINGNAG BOY

AND...
IDENTIFY YOURSELF
WELL...
I SEE
I WAS THINKING OF CALLING MYSELF... INCREDIBLE GIRL!!!
AND WHAT EXACTLY IS THE NATURE OF YOUR SUPER-POWER?

ZZZAAARROWWARPROOOOO

CAPTAIN ATOM! STOP THROWING THOSE HUGE CUT-OUT LETTERS IN THE AIR AND WATCH THE APPLICANT!

SORRY . . .

THERE!!!

YE – ES

THE BARONESS OF BIG BRISTOLS IS RIGHT···

GREEN AEROSOL! PROCEED WITH··· **THE** INITIATION CEREMONY!

AND IN A BLINDING FLASH, THE EMERALD SQUIRT KING HAS TRANSFORMED THE LEAGUE'S CONFERENCE ROOM INTO···

HAM BURGER CITY

RIGHT!!

KERPOWW

THE SUPREME TEST IS NOW READY FOR YOU, ***INCREDIBLE GIRL*** —SURVIVE THIS AND YOU WILL TRULY BE WORTHY OF THE LEAGUE OF SUPER-HEROES!!!

I THINK I'LL ··· ER ···
HAVE ONE OF **THESE**, PLEASE ···
IMPOSSIBLE !!!

YOU MEAN THEY'RE OFF ··· ?

I MEAN YOU'RE NOT ALLOWED TO **POIN**
AT THE MENU TO SHOW ME WHAT YOU WANT ···
YOU HAVE TO **TELL ME!!**

OH - RIGHT ··· A HAMBURGER THEN PLEASE
IT DOESN'T SAY **HAMBURGER** ON THE MENU DOES IT ··· ?

BUT WHAT DIFFERENCE DOES IT MAKE IF ···
HAM BURGER CITY

READ OUT WHAT IT SAYS!!

OH MY GOD ··· GULP
I'D LIKE ··· ONE ···
··· BEEFY BRUNCHBENDER

BEEFY WHAT, SIR?
ER ··· ··· BRUNCHBENDER

CAN'T HEAR YOU SIR
PLEASE! PLEASE DON'T MAKE ME!!!

SAY IT!

ONE··· BEEFY BRUNCHBENDER!
HAM BURGER CITY

IT'S "BEEEEEEEFY" SIR!!
IT'S GOT SEVEN "E"S!
AGAIN!!!

ONE BEEEFY BR···
NO!

THAT'S ONLY THREE E'S
SAY IT AGAIN

ONE
BEEEEEEEEFY
BRUNCHBENDER!!

NOW THE REST OF IT
NO! PLEASE!! NO!!

WHAT SORT OF SPINELESS CRETIN ARE YOU?
THROUGH THIS LOUDHAILER!!

WHY DO YOU DO THIS TO ME?
NOW!!
OH MY GOD, OH MY GOD! I'D LIKE ···
ONE BEEEEEEEEFY!!!!!!!! BRUNCHBENDER SMOTHERED IN KKRISPY FRIED ONION·· SWAMPED IN SUN RIPENED TOMMMATO SAUCE··· WITH YUM-YUMMY EGG-BURGER SAUSAGES AND A LUSCIOUS BAKED BEAN GRILL-O-FRY!!!

THANK YOU, SIR
TED! ANOTHER HAMBURGER ON TABLE FOUR···

THE WEST

Bragg Tonight I'd like to introduce probably the greatest living sculptor in the world: now in his eighties, yet still exploring new dimensions in the art he has popularised so magnificently during his lifetime - Sir Hartley Marsh. As I say, I'd *like* to introduce him, but unfortunately I'm not allowed to as he isn't a member of Equity. So instead, I have here a pimply-faced little extra who picked up fag-ends off the stage in Rep for six months, and also had the bones in his wrists removed, and is therefore qualified to join the Actors Union and moan about nobody giving him any work.

Extra *By saying this I have earnt £42.50.*

Bragg Quite. Now, Sir Hartley, in your work, which manifests such an amazing sensitivity in its translation of meaning from subject form to inherent material structure, how much was your primary technique influenced by, say, precursors such as Epstein, Zadkine and Brancusi?

Extra *By saying* this *I have earnt another £13.75.*

Bragg I see. Well, I'm afraid we don't seem to be getting very far with that interview; so while the pimply-faced little extra is being dismantled ready for his performance tomorrow in the shop window of a funeral parlour, let's move on now to my next guest: clean-up TV campaigner and viewers' watchdog, Mrs Mary Controversial-shows-publiciser. Mrs Controversial-shows-publiciser, I'm very pleased you were able to make it here tonight because I understand that while you were climbing out of the bath earlier today you accidentally looked in the mirror and censored yourself.

Mary *No.*

Bragg Now Mrs Controversial-shows-publiciser, you're quite well known for your rather strict views on morality. I gather, for example, that you once blew up a van that was carrying Oxo Cubes, because you claimed the name advertised Cross-your-heart bras.

Mary *No, that's quite untrue.*

Bragg Well that's really fascinating.

Mary *No it's not.*

Bragg No, you're right. It's not. And so we come now to my final guest of the evening - up-and-coming author and part-time dead rat, Mr Eric Pode of Croydon.

Croydon *Good evening.*

Bragg I think we'll leave that to the experts if you don't mind. Now, Mr Croydon, how have you been keeping?

Croydon *Embalming fluid.*

BANK SHOW

Bragg I see. Well, I'd like if I may, to take a look at your new book, which I see is entitled "The Reviled and Savage Fruits of Spring".

Croydon *Correct.*

Bragg . . . One of the things one notices almost immediately, Mr Croydon, is the somewhat *brief* nature of the work.

Croydon *I suppose it is a little bit short, yes.*

Bragg Just one word, in fact.

Croydon *Err . . . is it? I've never really counted.*

Bragg No, well I *have*, and I can assure you that it does in fact just tot up to one. Now don't you feel that at £4.95 in hardback, the word "Knockers" is a wee bit expensive?

Croydon *Well not really. I mean it's no more expensive than my last novel.*

Bragg Ah yes, your last novel. "Enthronéd in the Hearts of Kings". This, if my memory serves me correct, was about the same length.

Croydon *I believe it was, yes.*

Bragg One word.

Croydon *Yes.*

Bragg The word "Knickers".

Croydon *Correct. I wrote most of that one in Corfu three years ago. Obviously it took quite a bit of research, but I went into it quite deeply because I believe that - -*

Bragg I understand also, you moronic little twerp, that at present you are working on a third book.

Croydon *I am, yes.*

Bragg Now so far we've had "Knockers" and "Knickers". And I gather this one is designed to complete the trilogy.

Croydon *That's right, yes. "Knackery".*

Bragg "Knackery"?

Croydon *It's got a surprise ending.*

Bragg Mr Croydon, will you get your stringy little carcass out of here?

Croydon *Certainly.*

DECEMBER

31 Mon Bank Holiday Disney Time 6.40

Threw N.Y. Eve Party, and after that, up. Final attempt to sell something this year: sent off brilliant new literary work to Platypus Publishing Company...

Platypus Publishing Co.
Letter Heading Gags Ave.
Upper Hampton, Andover, Bristol
Nr. Nuneaton in Takeaways
Douglas-under-Terrace, Isla's Man.

Dear Mr Croydon,

Thank you for submitting to us your new work "Hamlet, Prince of Confused Finish to Anne's Husband in Scandanavia (seven letters)". Although this play had an undeniably original flavour I'm afraid some of the characters, notably Lord Chamberlain Spills Lion Soup (Eight Letters) and Place Genuine Reversal For His Son! (Seven Letters) seem a little clumsy to us. Added to which, the overall concept of converting a major Shakespearean work into a form that can be understood by crossword compilers, though of itself quite innovative, could, in our opinion, muster only limited interest on the mass book-buying market.

We would therefore beg to suggest that you might try another publishing company and I h
the Bisto people are said t
interested than we might b
at Andrex are looking for
pimply little skunk faced
pile of ordure and
sick in a bucket wh
bugger off at once
doorstep.

Yours

Platypus P

"HAMLET, PRINCE OF CONFUSED FINISH TO ANNE'S HUSBAND IN SCANDINAVIA (7 LETTERS)"

by Eric Pode of Croydon

SCENE ONE: ELSINORE

BERNARDO: 11 & 14. Mixed-up show in that place is a challenge! (4,5)

FRANCISCO: 4,6,12: 9,8,2,1-5. Horse denies it? Reply in Bermans were not you but a reversed printer's measure! Man pushing 500 won't sit, Dan muddles his conjunction to reveal old fun just as muddled! Second person, personally, makes a point in that pixie you own! (3,6,2: 5,3,6,8.)

BERNARDO: 7,10,13,3. Patriotic remark is not a short evil returned to the monarch . . . (4,4,3,4!)

Contd . . .)

1

ENTER
HORAT
a fresh
confined
(3,4.)
MARCI
poles and
indeed or not the done thing!
(2,3,4.)

(Quotation from *Hamlet*)
(6,9,3.)
(*Contd . . .*)

2

FRANC
Voice p
but neve
Ted.
(3,7,5.)
BERNI
birds do
mixed-up.

(*Contd. . .*)

3

MARC
Never c
Ancien

HORA
begone
death or

(*Contd . . .*)

4

11 TUES v. cold again...
frozen stiff in Tesco's. They'd run out of fish fingers.. Haaaaa.
12 WED Yesterday was Remembrance Day
Burst into song!! The Wurzels have commissioned me to write all the lyrics for their new L.P. !!!
Wurzels' Original Hits!
A selection of lyrics from the limitless repertoire of Somerset's famous singing group
BROWN MANURE
Ar oh-ar oh-ar-ar
Brown manure!
How come you spread so good.
Ar oh-ar oh-ar-ar
Brown manure!
Just like a lump of dung should.
SPREADING
Spreading
I am spreading
Lumps of dung
Across the sea
I am spreadin
Lumps of du
To be with y
To be free.
BLOWIN' IN THE WIND
How many lumps
Of dung must I spread
Before you can call him a man?
How many lumps
Of dung must I spread
Before you can call him a man?
Yes and how many lumps
Of dung must I spread
Before you can call him a man?
The answer, my friend,
Is blowin' in the wind.
The answer is blowin' in the wind.
SUNDAY GIRL
I know a girl
From a lonely street
Cold as ice-cream
But still as sweet
Spread your dung
Sunday girl
Hurry up hurry up
And spread your
MARY'S BOY CHILD
Long time ago in Bethlehem
So the Holy Bible says
Mary's boy child Jesus Christ
Spread dung on Christmas Day.
(CHORUS:)
Hark now hear the angels sing
Listen to what they say:
We'll spread our dung for evermore.
Oh-ar oh-ar oh-ay!
DON'T CRY FOR ME ARGENTINA
Written in 1956, but rejected, for lack of dung.
MY DUNG
And now
I've spread my dung
And so I face
ne final curtain
My friend
I'll say it clear
I'll spread my du
Of which I'm ce
DUNG SPREADER
Dung spreader
He's the man
The man with the lumps of dung
He humps the dung
such
An unsung spreader
With his fork
Spread dung
Merrily on high
Hosanna in excelsis
THE SPREADING DUNG OVERTURE
Spreading dung spreading dung spreading dung dung dung
Spreading dung spreading dung spreading dung dung dung
Spreading dung spreading dung spreading dung dung dung
Or-arr Oh-arr Oh-ay!
Hosanna in excelsis
And did those
Forks
In ancient times
Spread dung
FERNANDO
Can you spread the dung
Fernando?
(ETC.)
ALSO AVAILABLE:
"Come on, baby, spread my dung" . . . "I spread my dung in San Francisco" . . . "The dung has a thousand flies" . . . "Hallo, Dung Lovers" . . . "Something in the Air" . . . "What shall we do with the dung, then, sailor?"
AND MANY, MANY MORONS!

ENTERTAINMENT

Snifferies

EDDIE'S 24-HOUR ALL-NITE SNIFFERIE Greek St W.1.
Need something sniffed? Eddie's will accommodate you. Socks a speciality.
PRICES:
HAND-SNIFFED...How the bugger are we going to sniff things with our hands, you idiot?
NOSE-SNIFFED . . . 46p plus VAT.
No armpit too small.

CHEZ STREISAND Knightsbridge. Duffle-coats and up. For that Big Sniff Job you've been promising yourself. A wide range of objects sniffed to your own specifications.

Pencil Poking

ALBERY Air Conned.
THE SMASH-HIT MUSICAL
OLIVER
"Songs are an absolute joy" — *Telegraph*
"Sets and costumes took my breath away" — *H. Hobson, S. Times*
"A man comes down off the stage and pokes you in the eye with a pencil" — *Express*

AMBASSADORS cc 431-801
Harold Pinter's
THE HOMECOMING
Glenda Jackson, Gemma Jones, Marcel Marceau, A man who comes down and pokes you in the eye with a pencil, Tom Courtenay.

CAMBRIDGE cc 431-801
Ray Cooney & Mike Sambo's
NOT NOW DARLING
— "I laughed until I was poked in the eye with a pencil" — *Jack Tinker, D. Mail*

DRURY LANE

SWEENY TODD — THE PENCIL POKER OF FLEET STREET.

LYRIC Catford 1100cc.
ANNIE GET YOUR PENCIL
"Must end August 15th" — *RSPCP*

PHOENIX, Hindenberg
NO POKING YOU IN THE EYE WITH A PENCIL PLEASE, WE'RE BRITISH.
"Blinding wit" — *Morning Star*

ST MARTIN'S *Until you're sick of it*
YE MOUSETRAP
386th year!
with PAUL HAYES, JILL BURRIDGE, KEN REID, BOB RICHARDS, EAGLE HB, SANDRA WYATT-JONES.
We defy you to guess which one did it!

Non Pencil Poking

SHAFTESBURY
The smash hit
AN EVENING WITHOUT TOMMY STEELE
Breaking all box office records!

NATIONAL cc 431 801
OEDIPUS REX

VAUDEVILLE
OH CALCUTTA!
Phone 01 699 4221 to find out what they *do* poke you in the eye with . . .

Cults

THE HITCH HIKER'S GUIDE TO THE GALAXY has now been made into a LUMP OF WET PUTTY! for a limited season at the ICA. Meet MELVIN, THE ELECTRA-COMPLEXED CALCULATOR and the dull tedious man who plays the dull tedious man in PUTTY FORM! KNEAD all your favourite characters like ZOGGNIBROX BLARFLE-JUICE BRODZGR . . . ETC.

Snake Parlours

JULIE'S *VISITING SNAKAGE SERVICE.*
Your limbs removed and your body pummelled into a long sausage shape in the comfort of your own hotel room.
RING 431 801

AFTER YOUR FLIGHT or a hard day at the office why not have your jaws disjointed, extra ribs added and your tongue forked at **HONEY'S SNAKE PARLOUR.** Centrally heated tanks.

FOR THE tired executive in need of conversion to coiled oviparous reptilian form, why not call 431-801 now and relax as one of our beautiful snakeuses gets to work on your body?
SOPHISTO-SLIME — London's top-class Snakage service!

Travel

PYRENEAN TOURS Coast to coast by Lemon, only £76. Includes a full week's lemon trekking for two. Also return flights to **SRI LANKA, FAR EAST, SINGAPORE** by Tomato Ketchup. Simply book now and you will be stuck round the top of a bottle in a Wimpey Bar. Not noted for its quickness but you do avoid the crowds. Write now for further details to: THOROUGHLY RIDICULOUS & IMPRACTICAL TRAVEL SERVICES, A STALE PINEAPPLE, W.C.2.

For just £8.60 you can travel to Kenya by Reductio ad Absurdum. Simply reduce yourself to algebraic form and our trained mathematicians will prove by a series of logical paradoxes that you're arriving at Nairobi Airport.
Apply: THOROUGHLY RIDICULOUS, ETC.

LOWESTOFT

Jewel of the East

Features:
- Best ski-ing facilities in Suffolk. HAVE THE TIME OF YOUR LIFE IN ONE OF THE MANY AUSTRIAN VILLAS THAT NESTLE IN LOWESTOFT'S BREATHTAKING SNOW-CAPPED MOUNTAINS . . .
- Sunbathing AMONG THE PALM TREES AND COCONUT GROVES AROUND LOWESTOFT HARBOUR . . .
- Camel Rides EVERY AFTERNOON TO THE GREAT PYRAMIDS OF LOWESTOFT.
- Sight-seeing in THE EVENING TO TAKE IN THE AWE-INSPIRING GRAND CANYON OF TENNYSON ROAD, LOWESTOFT, BY MOONLIGHT. WRITE NOW TO: S. Letdown, The Lowestoft Not-entirely-truthtful Tourist Board, Hell, Suffolk.

Records

THE WURZELS' ORIGINAL HITS. A brand new LP to mark the first centennial of Deafness. Lyrics specially composed by Eric Pode of Croydon.

NOW SHOWING:
Kremlin 1 and 2

Albert R. Broccoli
and Hymie Green-stuff
present

"TO AFGHANISTAN WITH LOVE"

starring
ROGER MOORE
as
THE ACTRESS SAID TO THE BISHOP
VANESSA REDGRAVE
as
THE LACK OF SEX INTEREST
BERNARD LEE
as
USUAL

MARTIN BORMAN and HERMANN GOERING
present
A BORING-GERMAN FILM
Distributed throughout the world by
MARCHING INTO IT

The heart-rending tale of a Nazi Regime forced to flee the terror of a sickly family of singers . . .

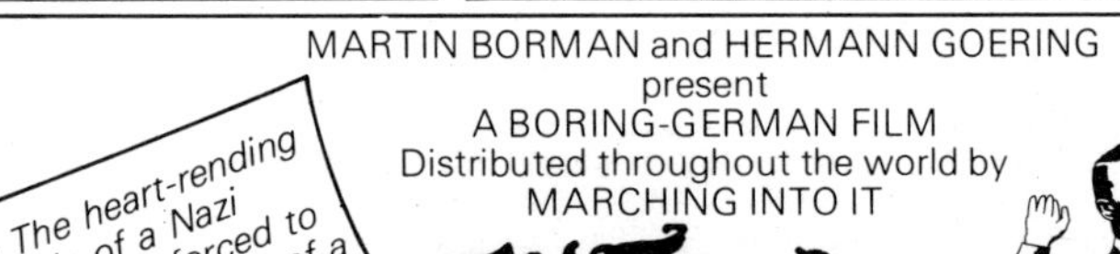

Songs:
"Bomb every mountain"
"How do you solve a problem like Poland?"
"My Favourite Blitz"

HEINRICH HIMMLER as SISTER MARIA
17th PANZER DIVISION as THE CHILDREN
JULIE ANDREWS as HIMSELF

Choreography by A GOOSE.

ABC BERLIN Plus: *"The Ten Kommandants."*

Cinecenta HAYMARKET Tel: 431 801
LEW GRADE presents
ROGET'S THESAURUS — THE MOVIE
starring, featuring, including, consisting of, embodying, implicating, constituting, encompassing
SIR ALEC GUINNESS STOUT PORTER
and also as well as additionally in conjunction with
PENELOPE KEITH RON KEVIN WALLY LES
written penned copied transcribed scribbled scrawled interlined composed indited by PETER MARK ROGET
Executive Producer LEW GRADE GOD DEITY JEHOVAH.

Exhibitions

OLYMPIA Until Sept. 4th

HE 59th INTERNATIONAL IDEAL BOTTY EXHIBITION

Wog botties, Frog botties, ago botties – they're all grist to the Botty Mill here! A REAL BACKSIDE BONANZA! POSTERIORS GALORE! LUTEUS MAXIMI BY THE TRUCKLOAD! *ALSO:* **APRICOTS IN SYRUP**

"out Japanese botties really. They've got a right cheek"
—*Mary Whitehouse*

Pointless Societies

AL SOCIETY FOR STICKING THE TERS S-P-R ONTO THE SPREGINGS OF SPRERTAIN WORDS

ore members needed urgently. Sprenroll now l sprelp us change words like MPLING, into SPRUMING, PIMPLE into SPRIME, Etc. S-P-R transfer ocations rely entirely on oluntary support. Spray us a t today.
Fruitcake Sp., Spreading.

Lavatories

NDERING what to do with *ur* lavatory this year? Why Go To It? Millions of ople all over Great Britain ve found that Going to the vatory is simple as can be, l very easy on the purse! No vious experience necessary. ite now to: The National vatory Advisory Service, tch End, Middlesex.

ATORIES are made for going Don't let YOUR lavatory vn — Go To It today! Further details from "Hatch-lav" The Cisterns, Langham eet, W1.

R YEARS I felt there was nething missing in my . . . Then one day a friend gested I go to the lavatory. ce then I've never looked k". So says Mr Vic Hatch BB-on-C. But don't take our d for it, try it for yourself. ther info in Lavatory News, ce 10p.

POLOGY

n early edition of last week's r we inadvertantly carried a rt stating that Lord Justice Dod- was an overweight yak whose n was punctured when he backed a cactus plant. We apologise sincerely for this unfortunate r, and for any embarrassment it have caused the yak community orthern Tibet.

Letters

'DUNG DISC' LYRICS:

A LOONY WRITES

Sir,

May I through your columns express my most profund indignation at the unmitigated filth currently permeating our air-waves in the form of a new LP penned, so I am led to understand, by a certain Eric Pode of Clapham. These songs are so disgusting I've half a mind to my certain knowledge. The full majesty of spreading dung is a very personal and sensitive experience that should be enjoyed only in private between a husband and his wife. In fact the couple who enjoy it between me and *my* wife are respectable in every way. The only means of curbing this explicit fertilisation is to bring back the birch in schools. And hang people from it.

Yours sincerely

Sir Edith St John-Surname (Retarded).

P.S. I have also sent a letter joined-up writing to the BBC asking for my fine as a TV licence dodger back. What these media boys need is a dose of National Service. It certainly taught *me* the meaning of the word disprin!

WHALE-CHANGE:

THE DECISION EVERY WOMAN MUST FACE...

Sirs,

I was appalled by the comments of R. Hackbenommto (Letters, March 3rd), regarding his wife's trans-cetacean tendencies. Like Mildred I myself was for many years unable to come to terms with the inadequacy I felt in my alloted role in life. Ever since I was a young girl I had suffered with the feeling that I was a large marine organism trapped inside a woman's body. And, like most men who are singularly insensitive to all but their own selfish obsessions, my husband simply did not understand. On one occasion he actually came home early, found me in the bedroom wearing two goldfish bowls, and simply complimented me on my see-through bra. Eventually I could take no more, and I resolved to leave him and have the operation I so desperately craved.

That was three years ago and I am now settling down extremely well in my new life as a whale. My blow-hole will never of course be fully functional, but I have found a truly understanding man now who accepts me as a 48-ton mass of blubber in a fully natural, caring way. Make no mistake: a whale-change *is* a very big step to take. But it must be faced up to in a responsible, adult fashion. Cheap, stubborn prejudices will get us nowhere.

Physeter catadon
(née Sheila)

YOUR PAPER IS

THE TOPS!!!

Dear Sir,

I am an elderly gentleman in his late 90's, and unable to get out of the house these days, due to a police dragnet. My one remaining pleasure is sandpapering my walking-stick, which reminds me of old times. Also, my wife Spot suffers from all sorts of terrible diseases and ailments, had to have her skull removed as a child, and now has both arms stapled to the floor for tax purposes. Despite all this she still buys your newspaper every single night. And hates it.

Yours geriatrically

Walter Sputum.

P.S. Since writing this letter I have collapsed dead, so please excuse surrealist quality of this last sentence.

NEWS IN BRIEF

• Joan Bakewell took film cameras to Wandsworth yesterday to ask how many people wanted a Free Press. Nine men appear in court on Monday.

• Top of the Pops producer Robbie Stale today announced he had contracted the Rolling Stones. He has been advised to stay in bed and lay off fatty foods.

• A man who was last night found asleep in Linda Lovelace's bed has been charged with loitering in a public place.

• A Black and White Minstrel was tomorrow run over by a steamroller outside the BBC TV Theatre in Puratory. Police are advising people to treat it as a zebra crossing.

• A member of the board of British Steel has died in his sleep. His family are claiming compensation for an industrial accident.

ADVERTISEMENT

From the makers of Old Stiff Embalming Fluid, STIFFCO Life Assurance, and Dorothy Stiffco Undersixfeetofwetdirtwear comes . . .
STIFF-COLA! The life-quenching drink from STIFFCO!

Deathmakingneverwakingoffpoppingcoffinshoppingitsnuffingoutofpuffingdaisypushingpetercushingnevergivingceasedliving.

Stiff-Ko

HEALTH FEARS
as leg-sawing craze grows

After months of extensive tests medical experts this week confirmed that the new passion among young people for sawing their legs off can, if left untreated, lead to serious health disorders.

Recent figures released by STUMP, the organisation formed to rehabilitate former leg-sawing addicts, reveal that in Britain today some 39,000 teenagers are currently the victims of this disturbing new social malaise. And it is a habit they find hard to kick.

One mother who knows the agony leg-sawing can bring is Mrs Phyllis Trodd of Southall.

"I was dusting out my Dennis's bedroom one day when I found this knee hidden under the pillow," said 38-year-old Phyllis, a dental receptionist whose hobbies are swimming, surfing and skiing. "At the time of course I never gave it a second thought. Then, a fortnight later, he came and asked me if I'd take up his trousers 38 inches. It was only then I realised the awful truth: my son was a de-legment addict."

Like Dennis, Ron finds that once you've started sawing your legs off it becomes very difficult to stop.

"I've been dropping pins now about eighteen months right?" he says. "We was all at this mate's house right and just for a laugh right a few of us starts cutting our toenails right. And it all just goes on from there . . ."

According to the police in Ely, some 230 youngsters regularly saw their legs off round the back of the gasworks. Others just above the knee.

But it doesn't end there.

'Normal-O': fears grow

'Normal-o', the normal-sized cockroach, la sighted eight weeks ago near the British Embassy Shepherds Bush, is now believed to be in th Shepherds Bush area.

Members of Scotland Yard's crack an cockroach unit have issued the following warni to the public: If you see Normal-o, do NOT sme yourself with mustard and lie down enticing between two slices of bread, as this may interpreted as an open invitation for it to eat yo Instead, call 999 and await help.

• Normal-o's escape follows last week's natio wide hunt for Not-quite-so-Normal-o, the ra Latvian non-existent cockroach of the ord Blatella Non-existicus, a species never before se in Britain.

1978:

The desperate years . . .

1978 marked a sudden decline in the fortunes of Croydon as a writer. In early January he adapted David Frost's bank statement into a screenplay for "Love Story", wrote a whodunnit based on an inland revenue officer's birth certificate, and began work on his new manual of rabbit breeding, "How to Make a Fast Buck". All were ruthlessly slated by publishers and subsequently returned with a brief note on the beneficial properties of ramming a privet hedge down his greasy little gullet. In February, whilst spending Easter with his Hollywood friends Swan and Edgar Lake, he began composing a new opera entitled "I Cavalletta Saliva" (The Locust Spit), and also an *old* opera of the same name. The action concerns a penurious grave-digger who is struggling to bring up a family of seven when his shovel breaks. His wife Boz renounces her love for him and runs off with Estragon, a one-legged beggar from Ealing who is trying to earn money selling Hindenberg souvenir books of matches. Determined to forge a new life for herself, Boz moves to Penge where she settles down, has five children, and then gets up again. But the affair is poisoned by envy. Tiring quickly of her amputee paramour, Boz finds herself falling in love with his other leg. Estragon's own leg, incensed at the cuckold, throws itself knee-first into a vat of stale haddocks and dies of loneliness. From there the story takes an unexpected turn as the seven dwarfs rush eagerly forward to kiss Snow White goodbye until she makes them stand on a chair. After they have gone to the mine Show White begins to feel sleepy and they have a whale of a time. The opera ends with 2,000 people demanding their money back. Sadly, the failure of this opus to arouse any glimmer of interest at Covent Garden, or anywhere else, led to Croydon's slow descent into the most desperately dire straits he had ever experienced. Unable to scrape a crust together any other way, he was forced to take on the lowliest, most embarrassing writings jobs known to man . . .

EMBARRASSING JOB 1: March 1978 – Croydon was employed by the Sucker's Digest Company to write ninety million circulars like this one for distribution in the South East of England.
Suckers Unlimite
Dear dear dear dear Dear dear
dear dear dear dear dear dear Dear dear
dear Dear dear dear dear dear dear dear dear
dear dear dear dear dear DEAR READER!!!!!!!!!!!!!!
CONGRATULATIONS SIR!!! The Gods have indeed smiled upon you this day, MR. His Holiness the Pope, my dear old friend!! Step right this way, oh truly fortunate one, for you are one of the selected residents in the Vatican area whom Dame Fortune has made her benefactor!! Yes yes yes yes indeedy!!! Tonight there will be much rejoicing at St. Peter's Square I'll be bound, as all your smiling, tousle-haired kiddies and radiant beautiful Curia toast your health in finest Champagne, chilled between the breasts of a lissom ITN newscaster, chanting merrily the lucky name of Ness the Pope !!! Yes, His Holi my friend, it's absolutely TRUE!! Oh yes yes yes yes yes yes yes yes yes yes yes yes yes yes yes yes yes yes yes yes yes yes yes yes yes yes yes yes yes yes yes yes yes yes yes yes yes yes yes yes yes yes yes yes yes yes yes yes no! YOU HAVE WON a fantastically lucky lucky break and a unique chance of a fantastic prize offered to you and you alone.
Make no MISTAKE, His Holi this is AN exclusive and unique number
selected. Your OWN PERSONAL hand-picked number IS -678D-98455
8946572837D8594-rT90577734343498F-099273746583748999
3049588872R-09f90-5559284759F95098-39iu839--444870
6473-C5A7T9-17N-H5E9LLS-CH8NCE-OF-W9NNING-HA
4k878-GREEDY-LITTLE-BASTA7RD/5555!!!! So, simp
right now and send off immediately for your very
Suckers Unlimited Book of the Gnat, a lavish leat
bound volume that will enrich your paltry home an
cause gasps of admiration from your friends and n
feet in total humiliatio
Read RIGHT NOW! this letter
IT COULD BE YOUR LUCKY
S60741A
THIS VOUCHER ENTITLES YOU TO GO TO BED WITH A NAKED LADY
OR WIN A LUXURY LEATHERETTE GILT-STYLE BOOKMARK
offer subject to availability
PLEASE SEND ME ANY OLD CODS YOU WISH TO OFFLOAD AND I WILL BUY IT!!! I AGREE TO BE BOUND BY THE ARTICLES AND ALSO BY THE HANDS & LEGS
Postage will be paid by you in the end because it's idiots like you who keep us going
CRETIN'S REPLY SERVICE
LICENCE No. JS172
2
The Suckers Un-Limited
GNAT Offer
Consumer Complaints Handling Dept.
Lambeth Crematorium
LONDON
ECS P1E
POSTAGE PAID (Special 20% Discount over 80 million)
S
TEAR OPEN AT ONCE!
or feel a right TWAT forever!!
open QUICKLY
OR YOU COULD MISS OUT ON THE CHANCE OF EVEN MORE EXCLAMATION MARKS!!!
Return the form in this envelope for –
A GUARANTEED CRUISE FOR TWO IN THE BAHAMAS!!
Yes the money all you people pay for our books will send at least two of our directors off on
THE HOLIDAY OF A LIFETIME
BOOK OF THE GNAT
MISS OUT ON AN OFFER LIKE THIS?
NO THANK YOU!
I'd sooner have my eyes poked out with a pen
NO THANK YOU
DELIVERY INSTRUCTIONS: ONE IN EVERY LETTER-BOX IN THE SOUTH-EAST PLEASE
DON'T MISS

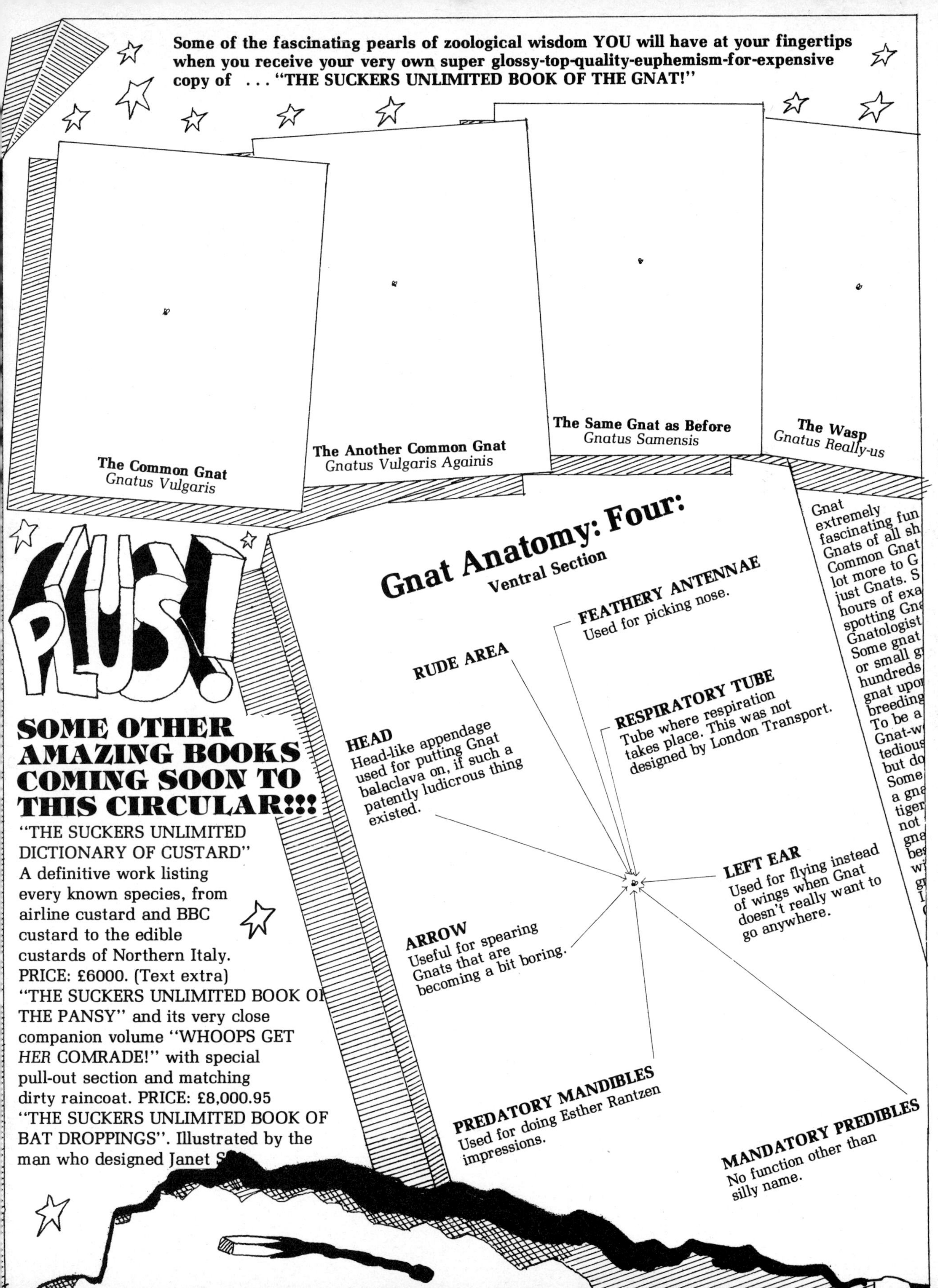

Some of the fascinating pearls of zoological wisdom YOU will have at your fingertips when you receive your very own super glossy-top-quality-euphemism-for-expensive copy of ... "THE SUCKERS UNLIMITED BOOK OF THE GNAT!"
The Common Gnat
Gnatus Vulgaris
The Another Common Gnat
Gnatus Vulgaris Againis
The Same Gnat as Before
Gnatus Samensis
The Wasp
Gnatus Really-us
PLUS!
SOME OTHER AMAZING BOOKS COMING SOON TO THIS CIRCULAR!!!
"THE SUCKERS UNLIMITED DICTIONARY OF CUSTARD"
A definitive work listing every known species, from airline custard and BBC custard to the edible custards of Northern Italy. PRICE: £6000. (Text extra)
"THE SUCKERS UNLIMITED BOOK OF THE PANSY" and its very close companion volume "WHOOPS GET HER COMRADE!" with special pull-out section and matching dirty raincoat. PRICE: £8,000.95
"THE SUCKERS UNLIMITED BOOK OF BAT DROPPINGS". Illustrated by the man who designed Janet S
Gnat Anatomy: Four:
Ventral Section
FEATHERY ANTENNAE
Used for picking nose.
RUDE AREA
RESPIRATORY TUBE
Tube where respiration takes place. This was not designed by London Transport.
HEAD
Head-like appendage used for putting Gnat balaclava on, if such a patently ludicrous thing existed.
LEFT EAR
Used for flying instead of wings when Gnat doesn't really want to go anywhere.
ARROW
Useful for spearing Gnats that are becoming a bit boring.
PREDATORY MANDIBLES
Used for doing Esther Rantzen impressions.
MANDATORY PREDIBLES
No function other than silly name.
Gnat
extremely
fascinating fun
Gnats of all sh
Common Gnat
lot more to G
just Gnats. S
hours of exa
spotting Gna
Gnatologist
Some gnat
or small g
hundreds
gnat upo
breeding
To be a
Gnat-w
tedious
but do
Some
a gna
tiger
not
gna
be
wi
g

COMMERCIAL ZP51098 - SHOOTING SCRIPT (FINAL)
Writer/Director: Eric Pode of Croydon

1\. CLOSE-SHOT
EINSTEIN STILL

VET'S VOICE: Einstein. Overturning the classical concepts of Newtonian physics he heralded in the frightening new age of Nuclear Fission. Our very view of the universe was shattered by his momentous equation connecting mass and energy .../

2\. ZOOM IN

But how long was his willie? /

3\. M.L.S.
MANDY ON DIVAN. FAVOUR LOW-CUT DRESS.

MANDY: Six and a half inches. Sometimes a quarter of an inch either way. But that was the average. /

4\. CAPTION SHOT: PAN. R.OVER. TITLE PAGE. FLASHING SUPER: "WE DID IT UNDER THE CYCLOTRON!!"

VET'S VOICE: Yes! All next week in The Tit you can read the astonishing story of Mandy Cow - for two years Einstein's secret mistress! For the first time ever she talks frankly about the size of the Nobel Prizewinner's private parts! /

5\. M.S. MANDY
/STAR FILTER OVER MOIST/
/ POUTING LIPS /

MANDY: He had this way of satisfying you completely in a very physical sense, whilst simultaneously jotting down calculations of perihelion planetary motion! /

6\. C.U. EYES

Boy, that really turned me on! /

7\. ROAM ACROSS PHOTO MONTAGE OF SCIENTISTS.
FLASHING SUPER: "HE TAUGHT ME THE REAL MEANING OF PLANCK'S CONSTANT!!"

VET'S VOICE: All in your sensational Tit! How Miss Cow met and became seduced by the entire nuclear physicist circle of the early 1900s!

Quantum mechanics theorist Max Planck! /

8\. 1-SHOT. MANDY, CUDDLING PLANCK PIC WHILE DRINKING CHAMPAGNE.

MANDY: With Max it was sex at first sight. Boy, he could really sell those five and three-eighths inches! /

9\. ROSTRUM ANIMATED GRAPHIC: PILLARS RISE UP FROM BOTTOM OF SCREEN ACCORDINGLY:

VET'S VOICE: Gregoria Ricci! Developer of Tensor Calculus...15.27 centimetres!
Enrico Fermi! Founder of subatomic bombardment ... 17.3 in the shade!
And Lord Ernest Rutherford! Key researcher into stable nuclides and alpha particle emissions ... the only scientist at the Cavendish laboratory with spring-loaded flies! /

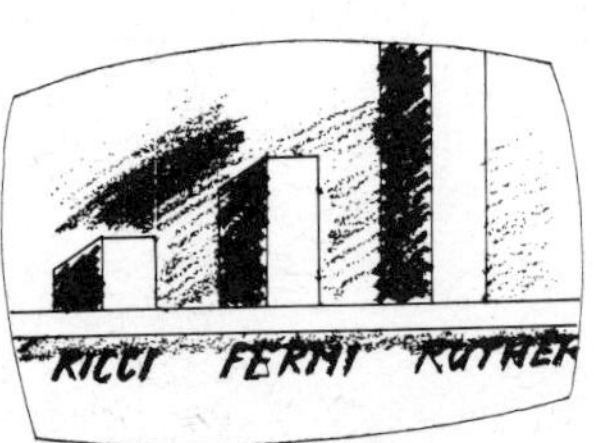

10\. PAN L. ACR. TITLE PAGE AGAIN.

VET'S VOICE: Plus! Also in this week's Tit! Your chance to win a super video recorder!!! /

11.	ROAM ACR. MULTI SPLIT-SCREEN. (NB: REMEMBER TO CHECK COPYRIGHT ON RONALD REAGAN PHOTO)	VET'S VOICE: Simply arrange these tits into alphabetical order and you could receive a VCR in your own home, so you can feast your eyes on all the tits, bosoms, bristols, mammaries, charlies and whoppers you want, day and night! Plus! /
12.	LONG TRACKING SHOT. (STOCK FOOTAGE, ORK.)	VET'S VOICE: Ludwig and Us! The Salzburg Philharmonic talk frankly about their torrid love affair with conductor Ludwig Podolsky! /
13.	33-SHOT. ORK. ON COUCH. FAVOUR WOODWINDS. /STAR FILTER OVER MOIST/ / POUTING OBOES. /	ORCHESTRA: He had us every night in the bath! He really knew how to satisfy a 33-piece symphony orchestra! /
14.	FLASHING CAPS: "PLUS!"	VET'S VOICE: Plus!! /
15.	C.U. BUDDHA BENEATH TREE. FLASHING CAPS: "SEX SEX SEX SEX SEX SEX SEX SEX!"	VET'S VOICE: Buddha and Me! Leading film mattress Debbie Trash talks candidly from her home in Bed Springs about the length of the Divine Gutama's naughties! Plus!!! /
16.	C.U. WHEELBARROWS FULL OF "TIT BANK ACCOUNT" CHEQUES	VET'S VOICE: Mazoomah and Us! ..... /
17.	WIDE S. GIRLS, ORK. REPORTERS, BANK MANAGERS ON COUCH. BANKNOTES FLUTTER IN FROM CEILING.	VET'S VOICE: Mandy Cow, Debbie Trash and the Salzburg Philharmonic talk candidly for the first time about the size of their bank balances after churning out cheap lies and drivel week after week! Yes, still only a farthing! The Tit - out now! /
18.	M.C.U. MAN WITH NEWSPAPER. CRAB L. OVER BREASTS HANGING OUT FROM IT.	MAN: I never knew there were so many in it! /

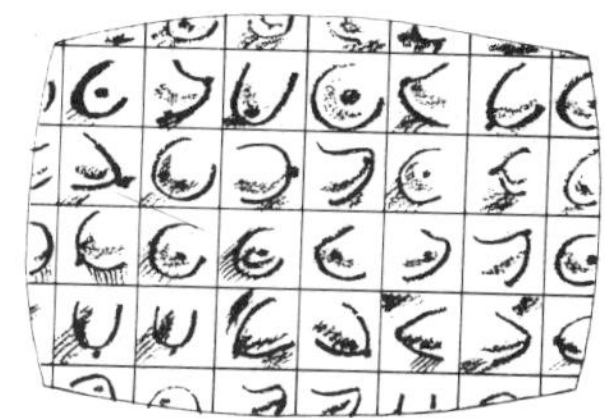

PROTECT and SURVIVE

AN H.M. GOVERNMENT HELPFUL FACTSHEET ON NUCLEAR HOLOCAUSTS

EMBARRASSING JO[illegible] In July Croydon did som[illegible] work updating this Govt. handout. For this he was given a free fallout shelter made from the corn flakes packet of his choice . . .

A Heartwarming Message from Sir William Celery Purse O.B.E.

Under-Secretary for Hours on End at the Home Office

HELLO there, Chummies! I am the chappie in charge of public information on Nuclear Holocausts. But our problems don't end there. Just lately I gather from the wallahs in charge of public opinion and the like, there's been a few teensy scares circulating among the world and his wife that nuclear war may be on the agenda very shortly. Some of these news bulletins appear to have had a touch of the old All Bran about them: chaps and chappesses running around gaga over the threat posed by atomic weaponry, as if their lives depended upon it. Apparently there was even one recent News at Ten job where that darkie with the drawn-on moustache had the bottle to suggest our civil defence ops were about as much use as a headache in a nun's dormitory. Didn't see it myself, because you can't get ITV down here in these bunkers. Well, all I can say is: trumped-up hogwash. I can tell you, *mes amis*, it cuts no truck with me about Red Rodney and his cronies hopping onto the Townsend Torensen to Blighty – and even if he did, what the bollocks? Two fingers to their silly fusion fireworks, that's my attitude. Listen, this Government has your interests properly safeguarded. I can promise you here and now that I and my colleagues here at the Min of Deaf are prepared to go on smoking pipes on nice lumpy armchairs for as long as it takes till you're thoroughly convinced you're safe. Listen further, staunch supporters: research clearly shows that even if we do sample a taste of the old "Nukers" . . . and wind up in a bit of a how-do with Harry Holocaust, it really doesn't matter. Five per cent of you *will survive*. Namely, your right nostril and the index finger of your left hand. So you *will* still be able to pick your nose. And that's a thought to take home with you, isn't it? Just put your feet up behind your corrugated cardboard screen (See Blue Peter 4.7.82), knock back a few of the old whispering benzines or a nog or two of Burton No. 5, and take a reccie at our little bookette here. Steer *well* clear of those niggly little radioactive dust particles that may try and gum up the atmosphere, keep your DNA spirals out of the road of genetic mutations, and Bob's your aunty. Piece of jam really, isn't it?

So there we are. Remember, if in doubt, it's always better to be safe than sorry. I know which I shall be.

Cheerie-bye there!

H.M. GOVERNMENT WARNING:
This man can seriously damage your health.

YOUR COUNTDOWN TIMETABLE

We must all be prepared if an atomic bomb is dropped at out door – as there'll be no ding-dong when *this* A-bomb's falling!!!! Instead, we British must be ready for it. So here's a minute by minute account of what to do.

SIX MINUTES before any future nuclear war, you'll hear this sound:

"There is no Danger Whatsoever of a nuclear War."

THREE MINUTES to go: Get onto your personal Parliamentary Private Secretary and have him unlock the secret lift to your concrete-lined radiation-proof MP's shelter four miles beneath the surface.

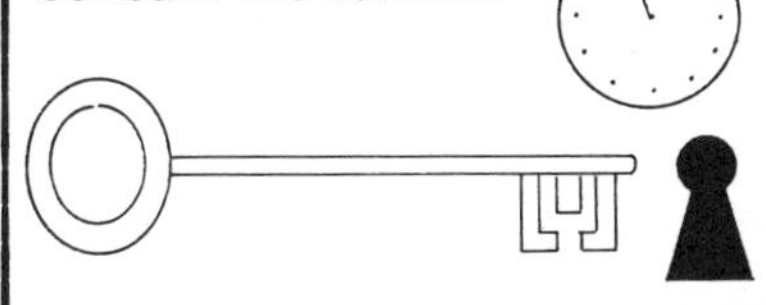

ONE MINUTE: Check your supplies of Personal House of Commons notepaper, library of Hansard, current draft legislation and pending Home Office memos, then sit back and enjoy it!

IMPORTANT: If you are *not* a High-Ranking Civil Servant or Minister in Her Majesty's Government, then it may be a bit more tricksy.

ALTERNATIVE METHOD FOR NON-MPs TO SURVIVE A NUCLEAR WAR:

1. Find yourself a nice safe seat.
2. Get yourself elected MP, join the Cabinet & become a Minister.
3. See above.

IF, HOWEVER, THERE IS *NO* HISTORY OF CONGENITAL MADNESS IN YOUR FAMILY, HERE IS A SPECIAL

EMERGENCY SURVIVAL PROCEDURE

1. Do *Not* run away. Stay at home in your house where the danger is greatest.

2.

Handles Handles

Build yourself an underground shelter of the type recommended by the Government. Get into the shelter and stay there until the attack is over. The major risk during this very dangerous period will be one of Fallout . . .

3.

Solid Teak

To make sure you *don't* fall out nail on the lid securely. Next, stop breathing at once, to conserve air. Once the attack is in progress the safest place for you to be is underground. About six feet under is best . . .

4.

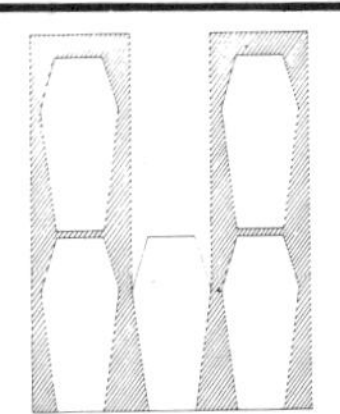

Get a friend to instal your shelter into position, in the prescribed upright manner. You are now in the best environment possible for an atomic war. Finally, an important word about rotting bodies. Wrap these securely in plastic bags and consign them to their rightful place: in the concrete-lined radiation-proof MP's shelter, four miles beneath the surface. (See Above.)

REMEMBER

PROTECT and SURVIVE

You can rely on your Government to do at least one of these.

Guide to the Galaxy. Haaaaa!

15 SUNDAY *Wimbledon fortnight* *Monsoon season begins*

Sent short play to L.W.T. All takes place in a Menswear Shop...

Good mroning.

Good mroning, can I help you?

Yes, I'd like to see a male assistant please.

I AM a male assistant, sir.

Yes I know, but I want to see a MALE assistant – get the drift?

Oh I see! Mr different-person!

Yes, Mr Same-person?

Serve this gentleman would you?

Certainly. Now sir, what is it you wish to purchase?

A pair of socks please.

I see, sir. And what size are you?

To the right.

I beg your pardon, sir?

To the right.

I . . . *don't* think I'm quite with you yet, sir.

Well put it this way, I incline towards the EASTERN hemisphere.

What?

I put all my eggs in the OFFSIDE basket.

???

Sir, how *long* did you want these socks?

Well, until they wear out.

I see. In that case I think we'll put you on this foot-measurer. Just give me your foot please.

(COUGH COUGH)

I beg your pardon?

(COUGH COUGH)

What did you do that for?

I'm sorry, I thought you wanted me to cough.

Sir, can we please confine this conversation to your *feet*.

Very well.

Now then, what colour?

Pale blue.

YOU KNOW FULL WELL I MEANT THE SOCKS!!!

I was TALKING about the socks.

Oh, sorry. The central heating's not working. Now if you'd just slip them on, see how they feel . . .

Hmm. They feel a bit LOOSE for a sock.

(SIGH) They're supposed to go on your *feet*, sir.

Are they?

Yes, sir.

In that case why have they got these elasticated tops on them?

Because you don't want them to fall down when it gets cold, do you?

I should say not. All right, I'll take them.

Thank you, sir, there's your receipt.

Just a second. These are for gentlemen who . . . well . . . to the LEFT, not the right at all.

What on earth are you talking about?

Look – that little symbol there!

That's a percentage sign!! Now will you get out of here you nasty, smutty little man and stop wasting my time!

Oh all right then. Good mroning.

Good *mroning!*

LWT
London Weekend Television
South Bank Television Centre
Kent House Upper Ground London SE1 9LT
Telephone: 01-261 3434
Telex: 918123 Cables: Weekendtel London SE1

Eric Pode of Croydon
Drawer Seventeen
Catford & District Mortuary
Stepney ST1 FF5.

August 20th 1978

Dear Sire,

Thankest in profusion for thy riggish submission concerning the mercer and his unmaster'd patron with the naughty quiddits!

An this company were demised such indign practice as to dally with commonty of this modern hue in sooth we were party to such a combination and should tarry not, but extend festinately this forgetive schedule of thine with its frippery full of girds and glances. Ye will construe i wis it is kindless for us to recoil with such garboils of the Twentieth Century, for any roynish ninny will unbolt to you our unwaver'd purpose: that the asserted portange of this particular company be to waver not from the enacture of period drama, the orgulous execution of which we do lackey journal.

Thus return we thy quatted serpigo, thou distemper'd whipster, that thou might perchance propend to a more precedent trifle presently, the better to suit our needs come the new season of programmes this Martlemas.

A pox on thy tercels,

Sally Seneca
Head reader, Drama,
London Weekend Television

encs.

described him as
generous old man who was
always putting himself out.
His cremation took six weeks.

21 FRIDAY Letter back from L.W.T. Coincidence!
I was just working on a new period drama! Starts with Q. Victoria struggling over the wording of a letter...

~~...Her Most Royal Highness, Queen Victoria, Sovereign of Great Britain and Ireland, Empress of India and of the British Dominions Beyond the Seas, Defender of the Faith~~

~~Dear Marge Proops,~~
~~You don't know me, but I have a rat~~

~~From: Mrs. Saxe Cöburg-Gotha.~~
~~Dear Marge Proops,~~
~~You don't know me, but I have a rat~~

~~From: "Worried Queen", Windsor.~~
~~Dear Marge Proops,~~
~~You don't know me, but I have a rat~~

From: Name and Address Supplied. (Sovereign of Great Britain and Ireland, Empress of India and etc etc.)

Dear Marge Proops,
You don't know me, but I have a rather intimate problem.
Whenever Albert and I are "alone", I am quite unable to find anyone to lie back and think of. I have tried Mrs. Edith Grint of Chingford, Vesta Tilley, and the man from the hairdressers' with the gold bracelet, but on these occasions Albert always seems to be a bit of a distraction.
I am wondering whether a crossword on the ceiling would be of any h... oh orbs!

Someone at
the door.....

Ah – Lord Tennyson. Come in . . .

Cor, too much, Your Squire. Very good of you to see me, know what I mean?

Er . . . yes. Lord Tennyson, I've been meaning to *talk* to you.

Oh yeah? Spit it out then, Your Tosh.

Well, it's about your latest work.

Oh right, right. The Morte D'Arthur. Nice little number innit? Real class job. Morte D'Arthur – Arthur's Mortuary that means, in foreign.

Yes. Well actually I'm afraid we don't like it.

Don't like it? Cor don't start coming that malarky, Your Squire. What's wrong with it?

Well look at it. It doesn't even rhyme. Listen: "Unless you cough up the readies by midnight, Albert gets the concrete leg-warmers."

It's a sonnet.

It is not a sonnet. A sonnet is something with fourteen lines in it.

Nah nah, you're thinking of Harold Pinter's last play. That's a sonnet all right, Your Guv'nor. Like that other one I wrote – The Lady of Shallott.

The Lady of Shallott?

Yeah, you know – "Out flew the web and floated wide, the mirror crack'd from side to side . . ."

That wasn't The Lady of Shallott!

It bloody was!

It bloody wa—— it was *not*. The Lady of Shallott was the one that went "Five thousand Gs or we'll send you more than Albert's ear in the envelope next time."

Oh yeah, so it was.

Quite frankly, Lord Tennyson, to my mind your work is becoming somewhat repetitive.

Repetitive? Repetitive? Repetitive?

Yes, and——

Repetitive?

I'm afraid so, Lord Tennyson.

All right then, Your Mush, I tell you what. Cop a read of this one. I was up all night composing this one. I calls it The Lotus Eaters.

Thank you . . let's see now. The Lotus Eaters, by Alfred Tennyson. . . . "In ones in a sack or Alby goes for a one-way float down the Thames." Hmmm . . . it doesn't really *scan* does it?

I'm a *Romantic*.

Lord Tennyson, get out.

Yes, Your Grandma.

Radio 3

7.30 *Stereo*
Mozart
Monotone Symphony Orchestra
conducted by WOLFGANG WOLFGANG
AYATOLLAH NO. 5 in Emaj (K267)
Six chocolate fingers
DIANE PENGUIN (*piano*)
(GRAMOPHONE RECORDS)

8.30* *Stereo*
Mozart
OPERA: THE SIX LIVES OF HENRY VIII
Sir John Right-Screamer (Soprano)
David Bass (Bass)
(GRAMOPHONE RECORDS)

9.45* *Stereo*
God, Aren't You Old Loonies Dead Yet?
THE MAGIC FLUTE
THE MAGIC CELLO
QUARTET FOR JEW'S HARP BUT TO YOU A TRIO (Op. 276)
(GRAMOPHONE RECORDS)

10.45 *Mono*
Mozart
PART 2
PAIR OF SOCKS
VEST
SUSPENDERS
(Sketchley)
Julia Brendel (Surf)
(GRAMOPHONE RECORDS)

11.55 *Old Series*
News
(GRAMOPHONE RECORDS)

11.80 *Black & White*
More News

12¾ am-∞

Test Match Special

DUET FOR WICKET
Ian Botham (Balls)
Richie Benaud (Ditto)
and the Fosters Chamber Piss Artists

Radio 4 YUK

200kHz/1500m
(*Holder: Sebastian Coe*)

Lord Robin Day . . . *The World at One* . . . 1.00 pm

It's no good looking here: we don't understand either

6.25 *Shopping Forecast*

6.30 East Anglia Today
namely Jan 4th 1742
Producers TWO MEN WHO DESERVE EACH OTHER

6.35 Today
John Timpson in LONDON
Brian Redhead in DELHI
Listeners in AGONY
including:
DENIS THATCHER's recent fact-finding mission to his wife's bedroom . . . is CHARLES WHEELER's head false? . . . Shooting Stars – would it improve Blankety-Blank?
6.45 *Thought for the Sop to Religious Broadcasts*
7.00 8.00 News read by ADOPTING A LUDICROUS OXBRIDGE ACCENT
7.45 Seven forty-five
7.50 Ten to Eight

8.45 A Book
read silently by SIR JOHN GIELGUD

9.5 *Stereo*
Stereo
A programme in stereo achieved by giving Richard Burton a single script to read.
(*First broadcast in extreme error*)

9.30 Start the Pre-written Bits
Richard Baker
KENNETH ROBINSON
FRITZ LANG
KENNETH ROBINSON again
MARGHANITA SPASSKY
A TOKEN MAN UNDER 50 with their own brand of whacky, witty looks sideways at the light-hearted slant on the inimitable brand of Radio Times billings.

11.5 *Stereo*
Thirty Minute Half Hour
(5: WALNUTS)
First broadcast on BBC Hendon

11.25 Pygmalion
by GEORGE BERNARD SHAW
A new production to celebrate his death.
Higgins ..... A MAN WHO CAN'T GET WORK ON TELEVISION
Liza ..... A FORMER ACTRESS
Henry Dolittle ..... HIGGINS
Pickering ..... HENRY DOLITTLE
Mrs Frost ..... THE KING
Passer-by ..... MRS HIGGINS
Mrs Higgins ..... MRS FROST
The King ..... PASSER-BY
Empress of Albania ..... GRAMOPHONE RECORDS
Producer BETTE DAVIS

11.55 *Stereo*
Sodomy Today
NANCY JONES with another dip into
(REST OF BILLING CUT)

12.25 *Wiggly Type*
Desert Island Discs
ERIC PODE OF CROYDON
Nasty little toerag presents his choice of records to the late ROY PLUMLEY.
Producer HORLICKS

12.26
Up Your Way
ITV Comedy executives talk about the constant pressures they feel.
(*Repeated in evidence at The Old Bailey, Mon. 10 am.*)

1.0 The World at One
Presenter ROBIN RAY
1.15 1.30 Latest mortgage rates

1.40 The Archers
(*For cast list see Radio Times Sept. 14th 1936*)

2.00 News and Mortgage Rate

2.2 Nurds Hour
with MONTEZUMA GREGGOR
Cookery: Arms & Legs for Teenage Parties.
DRUSILLA KNOX-BEESLEY reads something tedious.
THREE WOMEN WITH DANGLY EARRINGS spout patronising drivel.
FREDDIE "PENELOPE KEITH" DAVIES talks to Sonia Hyphens-Menopause about her role in the BBCshit show "To the Mannerisms Born".

3.0 Listen With One's Child Minder

3.15 Afternoon Bore
Two hours of droning rubbish some idiot got paid for.
(*Sir Penelope Keith is a jar of vapour rub at the Old Vic.*)

4.45 Short Story

4.45 News and Suicide Rate

4.47 News

5.0 PM
DAVE ARCHIPELAGO left-wing activist on The Socialist Aerosol and former editor of three policemen's faces, talks to JOAN BAKEWELL and after that, a brick wall.
5.50 Shipping forecast
(*Tidal wave only*)

6.0 Six O'Clock Newt
TWO SALAMANDERS AND AN AXOLOTL string you up too late on the latex world news and leather fircoats.
Edirot: CLINT MISPRINT

6.30 *Tridecimophonic*
The Hitch-hiker's Guide to the Galaxy
by A MAN WHOSE NAME OUR RELIGION PREVENTS US FROM PRINTING
Based on characters from AN UPSET SCRABBLE BOARD
Fit the Epileptic: Zodphlistblobbdroxvon and his hip chick Zilliablarxdronzdon together with Blodzigr . . . ETC.
(*Repeated: Ad Nauseam*)

7.0 News at Seven O'Clock
Up-to-date seven o'clock news from Seven O'Clock all over the country

7.5 Not the Bloody Archers Again, Surely?
Fraid so.

7.50* Asterisks Tonight
Starring His Holiness PENELOPE KEITH

8.0 News
Read by THE ARCHERS

8.5 The Archers
OMNIBUS EDITION
(*First broadcast*)

3.20 am
Week Ending
An irrelevant look back at some old Gilbert and Sullivan songs with worse lyrics.
Script by THE WORLD EXCEPT FOR WALTER THROBES OF PINNER.
Produced by A ROOKIE THEY DAREN'T LET LOOSE ON A REAL SHOW.
12.40 Shipping
(GRAMOPHONE RECORDS)

VHF only

6.0-12.40 am
It's East Anglia
Cowshed fu
for all the
farm wi
DICK J
CHR

DECEMBER 78
3 MONDAY *Bank Holiday* *Disney Time 7.13*

Went along for medical to appear on Desert Island Discs
Was pronounced clinically de
Relief! – for a moment, thou

1979–1980

The Watershed

In 1979 Eric Pode of Croydon was permanently hard up and had to wear loose-fitting trousers. Later, on 15 February, he went into voluntary liquidation and was emptied down a drain into a sewage outlet, where he met Barbara Cartland, then at work adapting her romantic novels into a form suitable for diabetics. For a few brief weeks Croydon stayed on as the driver of her face-lift truck before leaving to take a job with the Eastern Gas Board, spitting on letters of complaint. For Croydon these were times of profound disillusionment. His writings rejected; he spent a short time as a seedy entrepreneur in Soho. During this period strip-tease dancers were his bread and butter, until one day his wife caught him in the middle of a sandwich. Outraged, she left him for Sir Reginald Higgitts, the well-known elephant gynaecologist and pot-holer. And Sir Reginald left him for the dustman. Croydon's one-time business associate and personal lobotomist, Harry "Kneecaps" Saatchi, is alleged to have told Croydon that the chips were now down and he would either have to return to writing or starve. Croydon scoffed at this, and went on to prove he could do both. His somewhat unspectacular rejuvenation was marked by a ghost-written autobiography of The Devil, which he submitted in May 1979 to the world's greatest living impresario, Lord Russian-Émigré . . .

Russian-Émigré House

The Centre of All Creation, Chiswick

MINUTES OF A MEETING HELD 28.5.70

Present:- Lord Russian-Émigré Jr, several of his bank balances, a woman with large breasts and the word 'Secretary' stamped on her forehead, assorted Heads of State helping to hold up His Lordship's cigar.

1. MINUTES OF LAST MEETING. These were read out by the secretary while His Lordship gave the seat of his chair a suntan.

2. MATTERS ARISING FROM MINUTES. His Lordship stated that the rehearsals for the new production of Swan Lake were excellent, although he was a little worried the dance number might be too long. A telegram was to be dispatched to the Bee Gees warning them that the rental on the barbed-wire jockstraps was now up. Further, that failure to pay would result in the Middle One's chest being returned to the spot in front of His Lordship's fire where it came from.

3. ANY OTHER BUSINESS. His Lordship took a call on Eau de Nil that his two executive Yes Men were outside waiting to see His Lordship. They were accordingly granted an audience, and the conversation as is customary was recorded and transcribed as follows:

HIS LORDSHIP Come in, boys, pull up a Gentile. Everything going all right?

YES MAN ONE Yed.

HIS LORDSHIP What? I said, everything going all right?

YES MAN ONE Youse.

HIS LORDSHIP Youse? Yed? What is this?

YES MAN TWO Sorry sir, he's only a trainee Yes Man. He hasn't quite got the hang of it yet.

HIS LORDSHIP Never mind all that. I got this great idea for a new series.

YES MAN ONE Yes kidding!

HIS LORDSHIP	Shut up. There's this man, see, born in a stable. Big star overhead, shepherds and things. Then these three kings turn up bringing him beautiful gifts - at cost, naturally. Then he grows up, has these 12 followers, becomes ever so popular, until one day, at the height of it all ... he gets run over by a combine-harvester. Be dishonest, what do you think?
YES MAN TWO	Great!
HIS LORDSHIP	Came to me last night in the lavatory. And that's not all. I'm getting William Shakespeare in to write the script.
YES MAN ONE	But sir, isn't he dead?
HIS LORDSHIP	Money is no object. Then, for the title role, I see Elizabeth Taylor.
YES MAN TWO	I thought you said the hero was a man.
HIS LORDSHIP	Don't worry, I got a brother Hymie does great alterations. You know Demis Roussos?
YES MAN ONE	Yeb?
HIS LORDSHIP	Tessie O'Shea with a tuck. Now for the biggest thing yet. Guess who I got for the Three Kings?
YES MAN TWO	Who?
HIS LORDSHIP	Fred Astaire and Ginger Rogers!
	(A LONG PAUSE ON THE TAPE HERE)
HIS LORDSHIP	What's the matter? You don't think they're big enough?
YES MAN ONE	It's not that, sir ... but ... well ...
YES MAN TWO	There <u>are</u> only two of them, sir.
HIS LORDSHIP	You're right. No problem, no problem. I'll change the casting completely: they can be the Four Shepherds instead.

4. FURTHER BUSINESS. His Lordship then went on to discuss a new autobiography of The Devil by Eric Pode of Croydon, entitled "Soul Destroying Job". His Lordship said he wouldn't be able to read it for at least three weeks as he hadn't finished the On The Move course yet. It was therefore decided to publish it into a book, and he could read it then to see what he thought. A call was received saying that Bette Midler wished to see His Lordship over her two star parts. His Lordship suggested that she get a periscope then. The two executive Yes Men laughed so much the tears ran down their legs.

5. ADJOURNMENT. The meeting was adjourned at 11.00 hours and His Lordship retired to the Sauna to see if his stomach was done yet.

It is the Dawn of Creation - three years, two months and six days before the beginning of Time. Erich Von Daniken's publishers are just putting the finishing touches to their cave paintings of astronauts, and Max Bygraves is celebrating his first year in show business. But no one else is.

While the physical world is as yet void and without form, in Heaven God and His attendant angels reign supreme.

But it is not to last. For an ill wind is about to blast through Paradise, with far-reaching consequences for all of Mankind.

No one man was more inextricably connected with those turbulent years, and certainly none more qualified to present an unbiased, retrospective view of them, than Beëlzebub H. Lucifer III.

This is his story.

£8.95 drawback

RUSSIAN-ÉMIGRÉ BOOKS DIVISION

R II E

From: Art Department

To: Production

Herewith dust jacket for the Devil job. Have left out the line about Heaven being full of Rich Arabs who make a fortune selling extremely thin camels, because, quite frankly I don't understand it! If you want my candid opinion, I reckon we could be done for blasphemous libel on this one... You know how touchy Lord R.E.'s old man can be about His image. Anyway, leave it with you for now. Hope the wife's well.

-Yours is. [illegible] x.

I
CHAPTER
One Rotten Apple

"IN the Beginning there was the Word. And the Word was cut. So God created Heaven and Earth, but they still wouldn't let him say it. Then God said 'Let there be Doughnut.' And there was Doughnut. And God separated the creamy bits from the jammy bits, calling the creamy bits Day, and the jammy bits Working at Fords. Then God said 'Let the Doughnut bring forth swarms of flying telephones', and He said to the telephones, 'Be fruitful and multiply your numbers, especially on your computer-printed bills.' And it was so. Then God created David Frost's Global Village, and all manner of creeping things, and the creatures gambolled and balanced lemons on their ears and gargled with bound copies of Wisden's Almanac while listening to stereophonic creosote. And God looked at it and saw that it was not Good. In fact it was Too Bloody Silly for words . . ."

(Genesis I, attrib.)

ON APRIL 14 1970 Recurring BC, I joined the Paradise Administration as special angel to God. My duties in essence were to handle the legal arrangements for the Creation and try to negotiate a six-day week. One of the major difficulties at that time was that, under the existing proposals, evolution of multi-cellular organisms would take a vast period to complete, and this meant the huge world we were constructing would remain empty for many thousands of millions of years. In the event, the Hyams Scheme was rejected, in favour of a simpler plan whereby Man was formed from Dust, and Woman from a Vacuum Cleaner – thus giving rise to sex.

For something approaching my first six years there I only ever got to meet God on two occasions. He was always warm and friendly towards me and never anything but courteous; and yet somehow I always felt uneasy in His presence. He had, for example, many strange mannerisms. Very often, whilst performing a wonder, He would move in a mysterious way. Also, I once saw Him answer a prayer with the words "Wrong number". And, all in all, He presented a bleak picture, tramping restlessly about His office, head stooped, hands clasped roughly behind His back, His halo invariably failing to keep up with Him.

Cloistered as I was in my own unimposing little office three blocks away, I rarely experienced the glare of publicity enjoyed by my immediate superiors. Until, that is, one morning in the early summer of my seventh year.

I had left the house and was about to set off for work when I found one of my wings was flat. Having put it on charge and rented out a spare, it was something like 11 a.m. by the time I finally arrived at my office – only to find the place in an uproar. Every phone in the building seemed to be ringing, and my staff were dashing around in all directions, barking out "No comment" this way and that as they slammed down receivers on their hooks.

As I entered, Mary, my personal secretary, came hurrying up to me.

"Mr Lucifer, have you seen Genesis this morning?" She thrust a page of print at me. "Take a look at that – Verse Sixteen." Another phone rang. "Hallo, Mr Lucifer's office? No, I'm sorry, he has categorically no comment to make on that . . ."

What I saw before me on that paper I couldn't yet take in. Surely this was some kind of joke someone was having at my expense:

"APPLE-HOAX SNAKE WAS WORKING FOR TOP ANGEL. Anaconda on Forbidden Fruit charge claims: Lucifer authorised the whole operation."

"Mary, this is a downright libel!"

"You're not the only person they're tearing to shreds, sir. Think of the poor guy who was found with the naked girl."

"Didn't he get a good press?"

"We may never know."

Another phone rang. I answered it. It was Gabriel.

"I've read the reports, Lucifer, and I think we have to tread very carefully on this one. Find out how much hush money the anaconda's asking and pay it, you understand me?"

"But, Gabe! The whole caboodle is a pack of — —"

"No arguments, Lucifer. This snake has enough dope to blow us all wide open. If you value your career I suggest you do exactly as you're instructed. That's all."

The line went dead.

II
CHAPTER
Beware of the God

"AND on the First Day the Lord taketh He unto Himself a foot, and placeth He onto it an projection of flesh and of bone which riseth upwards to a point which is called the Kneecap. And it was good. And the Lord sayeth 'Why stop at the kneecap?' And the projection bore further of its seed and sprouted a thigh. And it too was good. And the thigh and the kneecap and the foot were the First Leg. And seeing the leg was not a Right leg the Lord sayeth 'Let this leg be a Left Leg.' And it was so. And the Lord taketh the Left Leg and set it amid that place which is called In. And the Lord sayeth 'Behold, it is good.' And behold, it *was* good. And the Lord sayeth 'I just said that.' And being contenteth in no wise with his works, the Lord took the Left Leg from out that place which is called In and set it forth amid that promised land which is called Out. And the Lord sayeth 'Behold, it is good.' And behold it *was* good. And the Lord sayeth 'Don't let's start all that again.' But yet the Lord was still not content, saying 'Behold, I have set forth the Left Leg in that place which is called In and that place which is called Out, yet am I not content.' And proceedeth He thenceforth to take the Left Leg and shake it all about. And behold, it was good."

(Second Book of Hokey-Cokey, XXXIV)

IN THE years which followed I found myself helplessly caught up in a web of corruption over which I had no control. Hardly a day passed that some new, damning revelation didn't emerge, casting grave doubts on the integrity of every angel in Heaven. In hindsight I realise the whole set-up in that den of rogues was tainted and perfidious to the core. Outrage piled upon outrage, fraud upon fraud, and my own protestations of innocence went unheeded against that sickening backdrop of moral turpitude. The culpability extended all the way up the ladder:

ARCHANGEL GABRIEL: former chief of seraphim, later indicted for conspiracy to plan the Garden of Eden break-in and subsequent fig-leaf cover-up.
ST PETER "CHUCK" ZERAPHON: former First Aide to God and chief adviser on matters of Heavenly Bliss; convicted for accepting kickbacks on the Pearly Gates, apple-bugging, and his part in the burglary of Adam's rib-cage.
J. GORDON URIEL: holy cherub on the committee for divine purity; implicated with former angelic aides J. Walter Ithuriel Jr and Daniel Mulciber in the misappropriation of harps for making bootleg lager; also later arraigned on a morals charge with a beast of the field.
MARTHA D. ST MICHAEL: seraph in charge of God's underwear, patron saint of piety, sanctity and special envoy to the Holy Trinity; convicted for wire-tapping, perjury, forging haloes from doughnuts, and embezzlement of eternal life.

MY OWN policy, as further scandals broke daily, was to do my utmost to maintain a low profile and hope things would blow over, trusting that my own probity in these matters would not be impugned. Yet I had not reckoned on the singular ruthlessness of the Man at the Top of the Tree. On December Twenty-one I received an official summons to the Oval Firmament.

"Uh, come in, Beël, how are you?"

"I'm fine, sir." I closed the door quietly behind me. At last, this was the opportunity I had been waiting for, to lay on the line my innocence in the whole sordid business. "Er, look, about this — —"

"I understand, Beël. This whole can of worms has been rebounding on your office, and what we have to do is stonewall on the complicity of the Divinity in this whole deal, you read me?"

"Er . . ."

"What I'm saying, Medammit, is the Eden rap could just blow through on the Bureau grapevine, provided these Genesis muck-rakers don't hunker down the blue chips or bug out with a hard row to hoe in any positive ballgame right now."

"Er . . . I'm sorry, sir?"

"In plain terms, Beël, we need to sever specifics from the compounded geometricality of the Paradise Pranksterism here, if they squeal the trumpet or come down antsy on the immunity question before we can stall the heat from the fish-bait in time and hypo on the beeper."

There was a long, long pause.

"Pardon?"

AT THE above meeting I was given to understand my position with the administration was safe. Then, three days later, in a special broadcast to the Kingdom of Heaven, came a bombshell for which even I had been unprepared:

"And I state emphatically, Gentlemen of the Old Testament, that I at no time had any knowledge of the Tree of Knowledge . . ."

I couldn't believe I was hearing right.

"Nor had I any prior suspicion that the snake in the Eden affair was acting under the instructions of a member of my own administration – an angel I'd come to trust and respect – Mr Beëlzebub Lucifer."

Was I imagining this broadcast? My brain reeled at the words I was hearing. How could He say such things He knew weren't true?

"Accordingly I have no alternative, to preserve the fidelity of the Executive, but to banish that employee immediately into a place of utter darkness – into the infernal regions of Pandemonium."

"No! NO!!!"

AFTER THAT, the world blacked out on me. When I finally resumed some blurred sense of consciousness it was as if a hundred eternities had passed me by. My mind was numbed by all that had happened. Slowly I opened my eyes to take in the singular suppurating surroundings to which I had now been consigned: the East End of Heaven.

My brain winced at the awfulness of it all: a seething, stench-ridden morass bereft of any scintilla of life or humanity. Out the corner of my eye I took in a sign which seemed to sum it all up.

"Heaven, East Eleven! Yes – H. E. One, One. From this day forth all the evil in the world shall be encompassed in that one single, hideous name . . ."

"Eric Pode of Croydon."

The words startled me.

"I don't think I've made your acquaintance."

"I'll fetch her later. I tell you, sir, this is the worst place in the world! The very Bowels of the Earth!!"

"It can't be that bad, surely."

"You wait till Opening Time."

"So this is Hell, is it?"

"That's right, sir. This is the place where they send people when they've committed a disgusting act of sin."

"And what was yours?"

"Same again, please."

"Tell me something, wizened, fetid little gatekeeper who art no oil painting, can you get a decent drink in this place?"

"'I have to be very careful about that, sir. If I fall asleep on duty fifty naked women come up and start whipping me."

"Oh dear. So what do you drink?"

"Horlicks. Haaaaaaaa . . . Exodus Three, Verse Nine."

Without doubt, this *was* the worst place in the world. I have been here ever since.

THE END

RUSSIAN-ÉMIGRÉ HOUSE
Fort Knox
Tax Dodge City
Zurich
Nr. Filthyrich
Switzerland
ALP 13

Dear Some Insignificant Little Toad or Other,

Just read "Soul Destroying Job" - liked it, liked it! Will buy and market subject to couple of tiny amendments: central character not sympathetic enough - is poss to make more lovable? - North Country vet, say. Heaven setting too remote - make more local - Yorkshire Dales for examp. Plot not gooey enough - suggest instead of clever satire drawing allegory between Watergate memoirs and Biblical folklore you have people shoving their arms up cows a lot. Public love this, I'm told - get them right up, in it as far as their shoulders - also wading through cow dung in wellingtons and fishing about inside diseased cats. But mainly exploit "arm up a cow" angle, I think. Huge potential here in paperback market, possible film and TV spin-offs too, so be a mensch and get to it already.

You are my obedient servant,

Lord

Lord Russian-Émigré
(dictated in his absence)

9 Sun

Came up with new Painting by numbers idea! Am rejecting it myself in order to save on postage...

"PAINTING BY NUMBERS" KIT No. 76: "Christmas Snow Scene."

KEY

1. Burnt Umber	5. Raw Sienna	9. Magenta
2. Prussian Blue	6. White	10. Scarlet
3. Yellow Ochre	7. Emerald green	11. Raw umber
4. Cadmium Orange	8. Vermilion	12. Sap green

No Bank in Particular
A Bloody Huge Monstrosity
Overlooking Pleas for Mercy
LONDON WC.

Eric Pode of Croydon
Up to His Neck
It.

9th October 1979

Dear Scum,

Thank you for your letter of the 7th inst. requesting a loan of one dustbin lid in order to give your children a roof over their heads. A propos of regard to the said loan, I have to inform you that your current standing with this bank is now as follows:

Deposit account	Nil
Current Account	Bugger All
Securities	What are they?
Collateral	Don't make me laugh
Credit rating	I.S.C.*

(* I should cocoa.)

You will observe from these figures that you are not so much considered a sound financial risk as a blot on the festering dung-heap of society. Further, I have to inform you that your personal account is now grossly in the red; in that you owe us nineteen pints of your blood. If this is not repaid in full by the end of the year, whoops brother, you'd better get on to the local Cremy and arrange an advance booking, follow our line of thought, sunshine?

Yours as ever,

Giant Despair

The Giant Despair
Executive Managing Director
No Bank in Particular

P.S. The quality of mercy is strained.

In the winter of 1979 Croydon faced imminent financial disaster and embarked on further last-ditch efforts to make a name for himself. In October he had the speech centres of his brain replaced by a jar of heavy-duty treacle in order to take part in a Radio Two sports programme, but was fired for refusing to cross the anaesthetists' picket line. This was followed in December by several other literary offerings which were submitted to the local fish and chip shop for consideration as wrapping paper . . .

SPORTS ROUND-UP

INTRODUCED BY JIMMY HILL

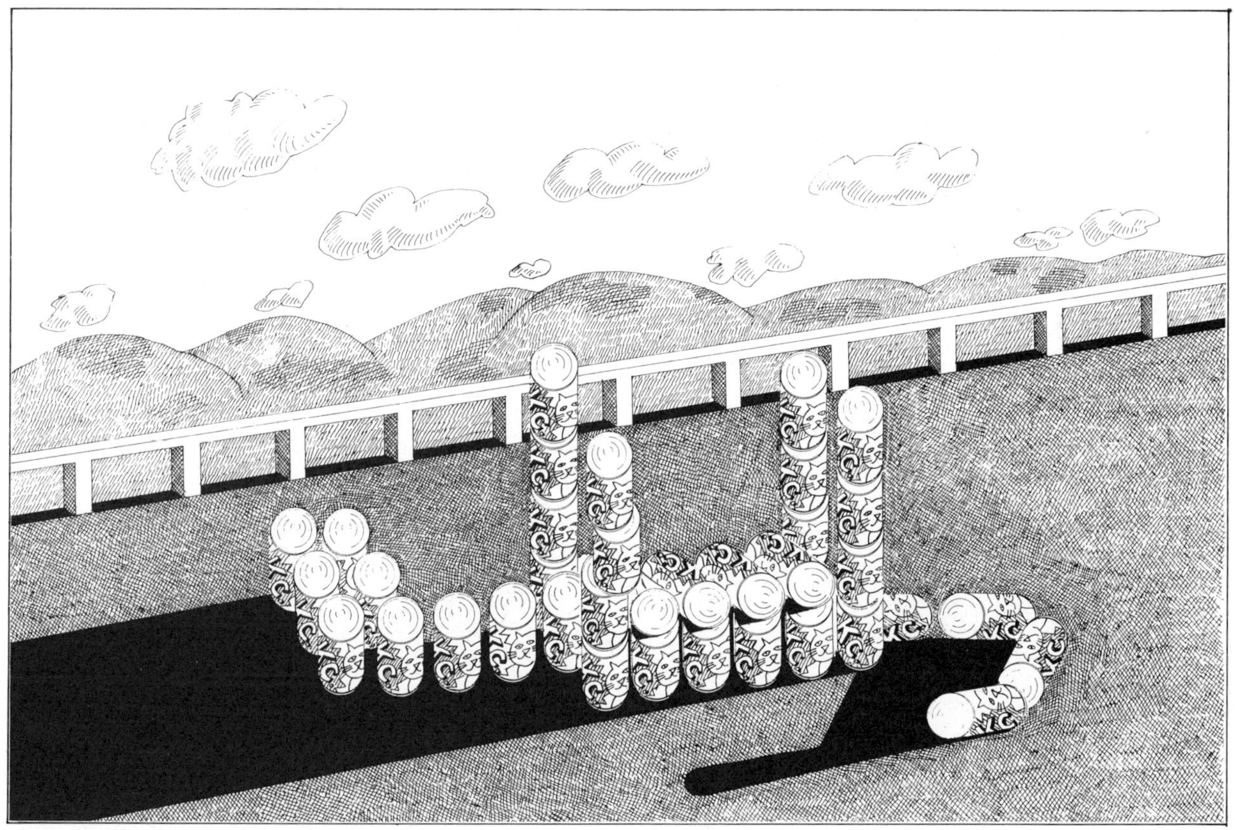

Former Derby winner Vanilla Mugabe . . . not tipped to do so well this year, following its recent sale to the Stepney Cat Meat Company.

Jimmy: Hallo, good afternoon and a host of platitudes to you. Well, in a really jam-packed edition of Sports Round-up this week we've got 500 packs of jam. We've also got all the headlines, scores and results you want to hear, plus 973 others. And in addition I can promise you at least one ludicrous-looking chin that strongly resembles a banana dipped in creosote. At half past three it'll be time for Racing from Doncaster, as that's the time Eddie Waring's arriving there; and then at 3.30 we're all going to sit and watch a load of horses tramp round and round a paddock for five hours, with a running commentary by our resident team of sawmills. That's followed at 10 p.m. by "Meet the Bitties", an in-depth analysis of the bits left on the floor of the paddock after a load of horses have tramped round and round it for five hours. This programme replaces Russell Harty, but no one is expected to notice. Then at 4 p.m. tomorrow we'll be going live to Aintree in good time for the 1989 Grand National where we'll be watching a load of horses tramp round and round a paddock for hours and hours and . . . (SHOOTS HIMSELF) . . . Ah, that's better. But first, over to Brian Balding for another edition of "On the Tonsil".

Brian Balding: A very good hallo to you from me, Brian Balding, and I'm just about to take my hat off, so stand by with the piece of smoked glass. And just a recap first of all on this week's "On The Tonsil": Muhammad Ali has now successfully stuffed into his mouth four mattresses, three wing-type armchairs and a horsehair sofa . . . er, but he still hasn't caught up with Brian Clough, who leads him by a roll of lino and two dead cocker spaniels. Oh, but here comes Ali again now! And what's this? This must surely be the most ambitious feat ever attempted! No, I don't think we've seen anything on such a gigantic scale as this ever before! I don't believe it – Ali is going to try and stuff his own head in his mouth! Well, this may take some years to complete, so in the meantime back to Frank in the studio. . .

Frank: Thankyou, Judith, and just a quick racing result hope that wasn't *too* quick for you. Next, we move on to our "Chess Poser" competition, in which, as you remember, we asked "Why is it that the various pieces in a chess set bear no resemblance to their names?" Well of course in fact they *do* bear a resemblance – and the first two correct entries came from Mrs E. Windsor of Buckingham Palace, and Sir Harold Wilson, of Studio 8, TV Centre, both of whom will be getting a 50 per cent share of the BBC's current defecit in premium bonds. But on quickly now to the World Bingo Championships, live from the Empire Ballroom, Orkney, where the first game is now in progress . . .

Bingo Caller: Eight and three – Number Eleven!
On its own – Fifty-six!
Tolstoy's barber – Number Four!
Up the Ganges – Deaf Thirty!
Slug with a handbag – Thirty-two!
Dead on arrival – Twenty seven!
Two little ducks – David Gower!
Political asylum – Number Ten!
An Irishman's gross – we all know that!
Was she worth it? – Eighteen months!

WOMAN: House!
CALLER: Check her card, Sid.
SID: Forty-one!
CALLER: No . . .
SID: Ninety-three!
CALLER: No . . .
SID: Eighteen!
CALLER: No . . .
SID: Sixty-seven!
CALLER: No . . .
SID: Twenty-five!
CALLER: No . . .
SID: Fifteen!
CALLER: No . . .
SID: Eighty-six!
CALLER: No . . .
SID: Seventy-two!
CALLER: No . . .
SID: Forty-nine!
CALLER: No . . .

Woman: I'll have the fluffy teddy bear and the goldfish in a bag please.

Caller: Get that silly cow out of here . . .
Age of consent – Sixteen!
Unlucky for some – Fifteen!
Back to the studio, and over to Dickie Davies – I wonder if it's true? . . .

East German weight-lifter Günther Pancake-similarity demonstrates her technique at White City Stadium.

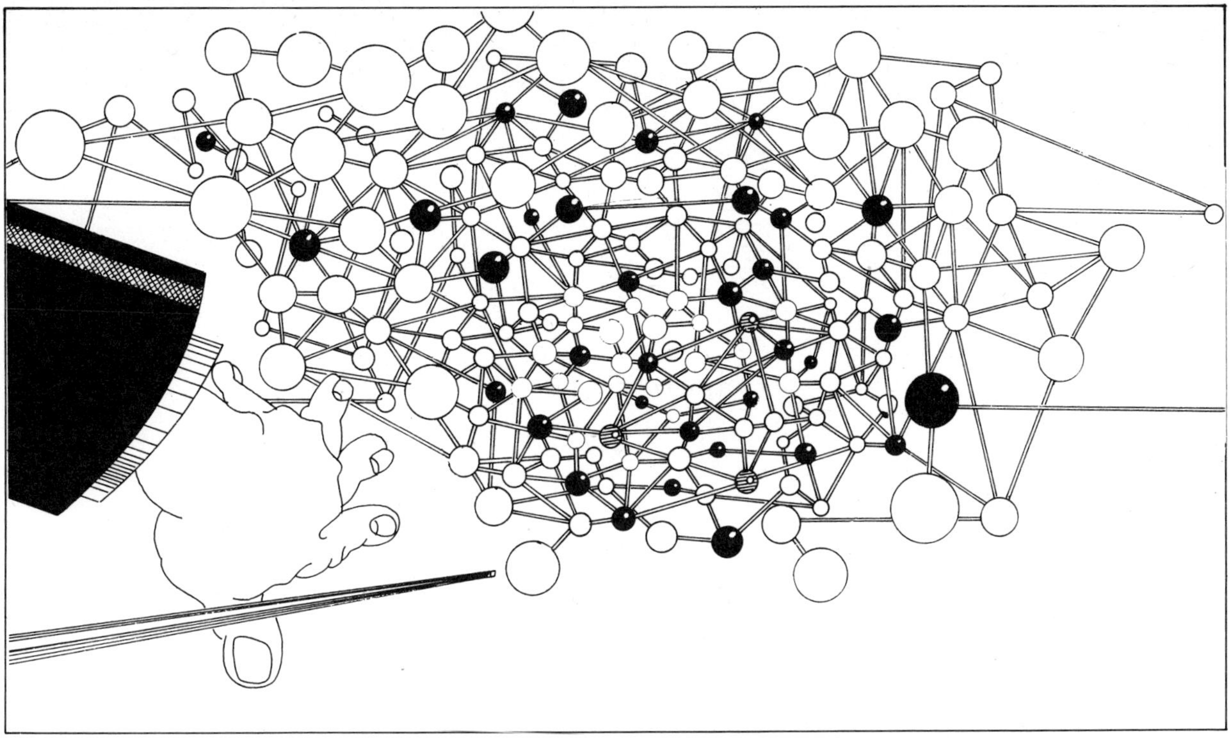

Ray Reardon goes for a mu-meson in the top pocket during the finals of this year's Pot Quark Championships.

Dickie: Thankyou, Angela, and we've just heard that there's been a disturbance among the crowd at Newcastle United's home match this afternoon – so straightaway let's join Fred Should-have-stuck-to-doing-How on the terraces.

Fred: Hallo, and this is Fred Yes-I-wish-I-*had*-stuck-to-doing-How, here at the Newcastle United Ground. And I've just managed in fact to get the crowd here to come over and talk to me. And your name, sir, is?

Pode: Eric Pode of Croydon.

Fred: Now I understand that earlier on there was a bit of a disturbance when part of you spilled over onto the pitch.

Pode: Yes, I've got a small unruly element.

Fred: Ha ha ha. And I understand you had a bit of trouble with a Bristol supporter.

Pode: I never wear one.

Fred: Ha ha ha. Isn't he a panic? Well, thank you very much there, Eric Pode of — —

Pode: I'm a rugby player myself. I play in the scrum for that Welsh team.

Fred: Wrexham?

Pode: It doesn't do them a lot of good. Haaaa. I got that one out of Bernard Manning's dustbin.

Fred: That sounds a bit risky.

Pode: It was, he was still wearing it.

Fred: Will you get your moth-ridden little cadaver out of here, you spotty . . . Ha ha ha. And that's all from Sports Round-up for this week, so from all of us here, goodbye!

Fitterati Schrickter in his new 3-litre Co-op FP Mk 2.

How to address people with Big Noses

An Archbishop with a Big Nose

Correct form of address:
"Blimey, My Lord Archbishop (or: Your Grace), that's a whopping great sniffer you've got there all right."

A Justice of the Peace with a Big Nose

Correct form of address:
"Your Worship, talk about Hooter City — and I've seen some conks in my time. Does Norris McWhirter know about that?" (Not commonly used when pleading for leniency).

A Baroness In Her Own Right with a Big Nose

Correct form of address:
"Your Ladyship (or: My Lady), that's a proboscis and a half you're saddled with there and no error. A Right Royal hankie-filler. (Sometimes abbreviated to: Rt. Roy.) I bet when you catch a cold it's a real Mount Etna job. Lord help us, ma'am. *Big?*"

A High Commissioner of The Commonwealth with a Big Nose

Correct form of address:
"Concorde isn't in it, Your Excellency."

A Queen with a Big Nose

Correct form of address:
"Your Most Royal and Gracious Majesty, what went wrong there, then?" (Afterwards, just "Schnozz").

A Cardinal of The Roman Catholic Church with a Big Nose

Correct form of address:
"Your Most Gracious Eminence, you *sure* you're not Jewish?"

ARCHIE'S FISH 'N' CHIPS
REJECT

A Coptic Pope with a Big Nose

Correct form of address:
"Your Most Sacred and Holy Devout Reverence, I am deeply honoured to meet you. Dennis! Come and have a look at this!"

A Princess of The Blood Royal with a Big Nose

Correct form of address:
"How's Mark?"

RIP VAN WINKLE

The man who slept for twenty years

Chapter One

Zzzzzzzzzzzzzzzzzzzzzzzzzzzzzzzzzzzzzzzzzzzzzz-zzzzzzzzzzzzzzzzzzzzzzzzzzzzzzzzzzzzzzzzzzzzz-zzzzzzzzzzzzzzzzzzzzzzzzzzzzzzzzzzzzzzzzzzzzz-zzzzzzzzzzzzzzzzzzzzzzzzzzzzzzzzzzzzzzzzzzzzz-zzzzzzzzzzzzzzzzzzzzzzzzzzzzzzzzzzzzzzzzzzzzz-zzzzzzzzzzzzzzzzzzzzzzzzzzzzzzzzzzzzzzzzzzzzz-zzzzzzzzzzzzzzzzzzzzzzzzzzzzzzzzzzzzzzzzzzzzzzzzzzzzzzz-zzzzzzzzzzzzzzzzzzzzzzzzzzzzzzzzzzzzzzzzzzzzzzzzzzzzzzz-zzzzzzzzzzzzzzzzzzzzzzzzzzzzzzzzzzzzzzzzzzzzzzzzzzzzzzz-zzzzzzzzzzzzzzzzzzzzz.

“Zzzzzzzzzzzzzzzzzzzzzzzzzzzzzzzzzzzzzzzzzzzzzzzzzz-zzzzzzzzzzzzzzzzzzzzzzzzzzzzzzzzzzzzzzzzzzzzzzzzzzzzzzz-zzzzzzzzzzzzzzzzzzzzzzzzzzzzzzzzzzzzzzzzzzzzzzzzzzzzzzz-zzzzzzzzzzzzzzzzzzzzzzzzzzzzzzzzzzzzzzzzzzzzzzzzzzzzzzz-zzzzzzzzz.

“Zzzzzzzzzzzzzzzzzzzzzzzzzzzzzzzzzzzzzzzzzzzzzzzzzz-zzzzzzzzzzzzzzzzzzzzzz. Zzzzzzzzzzzzzzzzzzzzzzzzzzzzzzzz-zzzzzzzzzzzzzzzzz. Zzzzzzzzzzzzzzzzzzzzzzzz.

“Zzzzzzzzzzzzzzzzzzzzzzzzzzzzzzzzzzzzzzzzzzzzzzzzzz-zzzzzzzzzzzzzzzzzzzzzzzzzzzzzzzzzzzzzzzzzzzzzzzzzzzzzzz-zzzzzzzzzzzzzzzzzzzzzzzzzzzzzzzzzzzzzzzzzzzzzzzzzzzzzzz-zzzzzzzzzzzzzzzzzzzzzzzzzzzzzzzzzzzzzzzzzzzzzzzzzzzzzzz-zzzzzzzzzzzzzzzzzzzzzzzzzzzzzzzzzzzzzzzzzzzzzzzzzzzzzzz-zzzzzzzzzzzzzzzzzzzzzzzzzzzzzzzzzzzzzzzzzzzzzzzzzzzzzzz-zzzzzzzzzzzzzzzzzzzzzzzzzzzzzzzzzzzzzzzzzzzzzzzzzzzzzzz-zzzzzzzzzzzzzzzzzzzzzzzzzzzzzzzzzzzzzzzzzzzzzzzzzzzzzzz-zzzzzzzzzzzzzzzzzzzzzzzzzzzzzzzzzzzzzzzzzzzzz.

“Zzz.

“Zzzzzzzzzzzzzzzzzzzzzzzzzzzzzzzzzzzzzzzzzzzzzzzzzz-zzzzzzzzzzzzzzzzzzzzzzzzzzzzzzzzzzzzzzzzzzzzzzzzzzzzzzz-zzzzzzzzzzzzzzzzzzzzzzzzzzzzzzzzzzzzzzzzzzzzzzzzzzzzzzz-zzzzzzzzzzzzzzzzzzzzzzzzzzzzzzzzzzzzzzzzzzzzzzzzzzzzzzz-zzzzzzzzzzzzzzzzzzzzzzzzzzzzzzzzzzzzzzzzzzzzzzzzzzzzzzz-zzzzzzzzzzzzzzzzzzzzzzzzzzzzzzzzzzzzzzzzzzzzzzzzzzzzzzz-zzzzzzzzzzzzzzzzzzzzzzzzzzzzzzzzzzzzzzzzzzzzzzzzzzzzzzz-zzzzzzzzzzzzzzzzzzzzzzzzzzzzzzzzzzzzzzzzzzzzzzzzzzzzzzz-zzzzzzzzzzzzzzzzzzzzzzzzzzzzzzzzzzzzzzzzzzzzzzzzzzzzzzz-

ARCHIE'S FISH 'N' CHIPS
REJECT

THE MASQUE OF THE RED DEATH

by Edgar Allen Pode of Croydon

IN THE dwindling hours of a cold, sullen day in the autumn of the year the wanderer found himself in a desolate stretch of country which was strangely unfamiliar to him. Ask not why it was that his spirits at once sank and his countenance assumed that lurid, ghastly pallor of the grave; for he could apply no rational definition to the sudden fear which gripped him body and soul. Something singularly oppressive seemed to taint the rank air which hung beneath those pallid tree trunks, crumbling and cowering, bearing in their sombre misshapen branches the inimitable augur of Death.

As the leaden clouds thickened across the grey sky he was seized with an almost tangible dread at the funereal mien of his new encompassment. A desire to turn and flee fell smothered beneath that unrelieved sense of horror and despair which keeps a man in panic rooted to the spot.

Throughout a long, long passage of time his frozen form made neither progress forward nor retreat. Yet, though his tortured eyes had for many minutes been obdurately closed lest they should look further upon that doleful vista, he was presently possessed of the acute sensation that he was no longer alone. And now the awful truth was acknowledged. A presence yet more dreadful than any hideous phantasm his delerious brain could have conjured up stood there before him: with its grim, unmistakeable visage faced him, and thus addressed him:

"Ho there, wizened old man!"

"Pardon me?"

"I said, Ho there, wizened old man, gathering wooden logs to bring a meagre spark of warmth to his racked old body."

"I beg yours?"

"You *are* a wizened old man gathering wooden logs to bring a meagre spark of warmth to his racked old body, aren't you?"

"Not me, no."

"What's this you're carrying then, Burt Lancaster's toothpicks? Know you not in whose morbid presence you now stand, miserable wretch? I am the Hooded Figure of Death!"

"Sorry, I've already voted."

"What?"

"I've already voted."

"What are you talking about?"

"Aren't you canvassing for the Tory Party?"

"Look! I am DEATH! I am the awesome apocalyptic personage of the ultimate reaper of souls, harbinger of mortal termination, and general snuffer of life!!! And I finished canvassing for the Tory Party *weeks* ago! Now don't muck me about, buster, the hour is up, the warrant signed; the sands of Time have run their course. I, Death, have come for you."

The dread lineaments of the phantom transmuted into an aspect yet more repellant than before as its dismal form advanced upon the wayfarer. For the moment was now arrived. The Ultimate Horror from whose inevitable sentence all men shrink was now to descend in a wreath of cloying nausea to exact that final due which it must claim from us all.

Bang!

A heavy sepulchral silence tenanted the gloomy hilltop. No leaf or stone dared intrude upon the still, stark solemnity with its tremor.

"Huh! I didn't think much of *that.*"

"What?"

"Well it was pretty damned banal, wasn't it - just shooting me."

"What do you mean - it's Death, isn't it?"

"I'd expected something a bit more mystical."

"Oh I see. We'd like it a bit more mystical would we? Been watching Ingmar Bergman again, have we? Pardon *me* while I wipe my nose! You awkward, uncooperative little ponce! Lie down and stop breathing at once! You're supposed to be a corpse!"

"No, I don't fancy that."

"Don't *fancy* it? You haven't got any bleeding choice, mate. You're dead!"

"No, it's really not my cup of tea - sorry and all that. Now if you'll just excuse me . . ."

"All right! All *right*! I'll tell you what I'll do. I have a proposition. Take *this* back to your village and I'll let you off."

"What is it?"

"Its name is . . . The Red Death! A horrible putrid plague that brings a festering misery and abominable blight upon the whole of humanity!"

"Nicholas who?"

"Just take it and go before I lose my sodding temper . . ."

And thus was delivered unto the land the fatal contagion. And the spectre's prophecy found odious fulfilment. For pestilence and devastation were the hideous hallmarks of the Red Death as it decimated the region. And for months the disease ravaged the kingdom, and the name of its survivors was none.

Yet the Prince Prospero had escaped all encounter with the deadly sickness. And caring nought for those who resided in his deleterious domain he sought refuge for himself in a far-off castellated abbey. Here, the locks on the huge, lofty gates were at once forged and welded together, and the padlocks of adamant further secured with chains of wrought-iron. And to eliminate finally any chance that they might be opened they were lifted off their hinges and cast into the river.

The morbid afflictions of the Red Death thus consigned to the outside world, Prospero and his courtiers proceeded to make merry with the most grotesque and fanciful masquerade of all time.

It was a revel of the most bizarre nature; indulgence and concupiscence manifested in all manner of wanton eccentricity. But more bizarre still was the unusual suite of rooms in which the Masque was staged. For each, though outwardly dispensing the effect of a normal chamber, was so fashioned as to house certain machinery of the burlesque, allowing all who ventured through to disport themselves by means of its waggish appurtenances.

The chamber at the eastern extremity, for instance, was host to eight wonderful little constructions whose singular manner of design miraculously synthesised the physiognomy of a fried egg. And yet the bluff of the ovoid mummery was so difficult to detect that a thousand japes were effected at the expense of those courtiers who entered with no suspicion of any knavery. In the adjoining apartment, moreover, there stood an ablution receptacle which housed an unguent of a most comic nature, the consequence of whose application to the visage was a transfiguration from its natural hue to that of deepest ebony, affording conjugate drollery among the attendant assembly.

In conjunction with these two galleries was sited a further hall which exhibited an even more ingenious artifice of quip: a confection of seemingly innocuous guise, so engineered within its packaging that, upon removal for the purposes of mastication, the digits of the individual became sharply and inextricably ensnared; the instrument of dupe labouring, as I believe, under the cognomen of "Snappy Chewing Gum".

And the deeper one advanced into the set of rooms the more outrageous grew the extravagant trappings of buffoonery: a missile of the Long Bow with which the prankster could so accoutre his head as to give credence to the tenet that it had totally penetrated his skull; a cigar whose innocent ignition effected an explosive discharge of incompatible violence; a squirty button-hole; joy buzzers - hours of fun; X-Ray Spex and whoopee cushions emitting a real Bronx cheer; "Buggy Ice Cubes"; red-hot pepper gum - it's too funny! and plastic dogs' whoopsies - just like Fido's own!

"Avalanche" shaving cream - ordinary looking can, but one press means one big mess! Spud gun - fires 100 potato pellets a minute; Hypno-coin - amaze your friends; Phony arm cast - looks like the real thing, just twenty-five cents; "Clickety Clack", the *original* talking teeth! Exploding pineapple - give Mum a fright she'll never forget! Stink loads - two dimes a pack of fifty; Seebackcroscope and "Ventrillo" - only *you*'ll know how it's done!

Now when the Masque was at its height, and the revellers engrossed in every excess of pruriency and Bacchanalia, there came to the attention of those present, one by one, a strange hooded figure in their midst. What it was in his arresting demeanour which chilled the blood of the whole company no soul who was not there in that room will ever be able to conjecture. Suffice to assert that within a single minute the gaiety of the occasion had completely evaporated like a ghost in the night, and the eye of every single individual now was focused in unaccountable dismay on the masked stranger.

The countenance of even Prince Prospero paled to alabaster as he made approach towards his unheralded guest. For the Truth which was too abhorrent to contemplate slowly began to dawn, and a suffusion of helpless, mortal fear took violent possession over every part of his being.

"Stay my misery, you evil cur! Have you no tongue in that foul, rotting head of yours? Speak to me! Your name, you beast - tell me your name!"

"You know well enough who *I* am, Prince Prospero."

The words froze upon the air like chips of ice.

"I feared it. Torture me no more. You are of course . . . Death!"

"No."

"What do you mean, No?"

"Death couldn't make it, I'm afraid. He's playing in goal for Chelsea tonight. I'm his deputy, Sniffly Dose."

"Sniffly Nose?"

"Yes. I'm not *quite* as frightening as Death, but I can be pretty vicious when I'm riled. Listen: Ha . . . ha . . . ha. Evil Prospero! Thought you that you could cloister yourself in this castle and escape your destiny? There is doe ban alive can give Sniffly Dose the slip! Ha ha h - - Prospero? Prospero! . . . Where did he go?"

In vain did Prospero flee for his very life. For the hideous presence which had descended upon the abbey stole among them now, and one by one they fell prostrate in slight nasal congestion. Trapped within the tomb they themselves had fashioned did they fall prey to the snuffles, and everywhere throughout the vaulted recesses of the castle were dabbed paper hankies to moist nostrils.

And catarrh came finally to the sinuses of Prince Prospero. And the occasional sneeze reverberated along his grim and gloomy corridors. And the olfactory organs of everyone did they tingle and get a bit runny. And the snuffling and sniffling of Sniffly Nose held illimitable dominion over all.

THIS WEEK THE PRESIDENT OF THE UNITED STATES GOT UP FOR THE FIRST TIME SINCE ASSUMING OFFICE. NOW STATESMAN'S AMERICAN CORRESPONDENT SPOKE TO HIM ABOUT THE GROWING TENSION IN EAST-WEST RELATIONS.

NS: Mr President, a number of people have recently called into question your ability to govern in the present crisis.

PRESIDENT: Baaaaaaaaaaaaaaaaaapp!

How do you react to this criticism?

Baaaaaaaaaaaaaaaaaaapp!

Mr President?

Who said that? Who said what? *That.*

Er . . . I did, sir.

Oh, did I? Fine. Now then, how long is it exactly since you took office now?

No, No, you're the President, sir.

Am I? Yes, you are. Oh, I do beg your pardon. I have this little personal problem, you see. **Personal problem?** Yes, I am unable to tell myself apart from other people. It's nothing to worry about.

I wish you wouldn't use my typeface like that, Sir.

Oh, I'm sorry . . .

Mr President!

I do beg your pardon.

So apart from that you're completely normal.

Apart from that I am wholly normal and I Baaaaaaaaaaaaaaaap! have no other trouble of Baaaaaaaaaaaaaaaaap! any sort – apart from occasionally going Baaaaaaaaaaaa – aaap! now and again, and I fully resent any slur on my capacity to decide the entire fate of mankind. I see. Then let me move on to my next question, sir . . .

I believe that, as a response to the ever-worsening situation in the Gulf States you gave the order this morning for something to be dropped on Saudi Arabia.

Correct, yes.

What was it?

Baaaaaaaaaaaaaaaaaaapp!

Mr President?

Yes?

What *was* it?

Oh. Well, it was kind of large, somewhat rounded in shape, with a sort of point at one end, and with, er, yellow spots – well, more sort of vibrant magnolia in reality – you know that colour that is very popular for behind the desks on current affairs programs . . . Green I think it's called, and it had thirteen long floppy pieces dropping from the handles in the middle with a huge wedge-shaped thing on top, short triangular wobbly bits, and some lozenge-shaped strips of something rather wet and messy, and a series of big bulbous furry objects set into each side in a kind of interesting croissant motif, with sparkly bits cascading from out one of the long projections at the left-hand side, and a series of red metal cubes arranged in a helical formation just below the long matrix of gold studs that are set along the hull, and big wings – ever so big, in heavy titanium, with dangling strips of orange stuff coming out at one-metre intervals. And a US insignia on the side.

I see. And you've no idea at all what it was?

None whatever. But Mrs Thatcher has given it her full backing.

WHO'S WHO IN THE POWER STAKES . . .

The President of the USA is just one of many leading world statesmen who have now gone completely loopy. Eric Pode of Croydon looks at some others.

Dung Xiao-Fung, commander-in-chief of over 7 million Chinese atomic warfare units suffers from severe syntatic problems. At the age of four he got his nose stuck up his finger and used to beat his mother with a limp of stick celery. Mrs Thatcher has given him her full backing.

President Kung See Loo of the Dominican Republic believes God is a chartered surveyor, sucks the colours off Smarties in his spare time, and was happily married to a piano for almost 18 serious injuries. He has promised, if re-elected, to eat the Greek Orthodox Church without mayonnaise. Mrs Thatcher has given him her full backing.

Emperor Julius Ro'Boto of te Central African Emirate, currently developing their own intercontinental ballistic missile force, is a large deep twist-pile Axminster in easycare Acrilan fibre. Despite this he has ordered 48 million death sentences in Great Britain alone. Mrs Thatcher has given him her foam backing.

President Dub Gung Dee-Doo of the South-Western Woo Woo Bareesh can go Waaaaaak for almost three minutes. Questioned on the rationale of his new cruise missile force, he

(Turn to page 42)

578 H /19003 MEDICAL REPORT

DATED 1st Jan 1980	PATIENT'S NAME Croydon, Eric Pode of.
REASON FOR EXAMINATION General debilitation.	BLOOD GROUP TIZER.

DOCTOR: Just a few details, Mr Croydon - are you married?

PODE: Yes, I got a wife weighs $33\frac{1}{2}$ stone.

DOCTOR: And do you have a job?

PODE: I find it impossible.

DOCTOR: Where are you living at the moment?

PODE: Just above the waist.

DOCTOR: Fine ... Wide open ...

PODE: Sorry, I'll do them up.

DOCTOR: Have you ever been inoculated?

PODE: Yes.

DOCTOR: Against what?

PODE: A wall.

DOCTOR: And what do you do for a living?

PODE: Breathe.

DOCTOR: Children?

PODE: No thanks.

DOCTOR: Right put them on again, Miss Crabtree. Now then, Mr Croydon, quite frankly the one-liners seem in excellent shape, considering their age. I think you've probably just been worrying too much.

PODE: Give it to me straight, doctor. How long have I got?

DOCTOR: I'ts hard to tell from this angle. Personally I'd say that providing you stick to a well-balanced diet, don't smoke, get plenty of regular exercise and stay fit you've got another fifteen, maybe even twenty left yet. Maybe even half an hour.

PODE: Thank you doctor.

DOCTOR: Off you go then, and remember don't overdo things. They do say too much of it can make you go deaf.

PODE: Too much of what?

DOCTOR: Pardon?

16 Wed
Ash Wednesday

First day of Lent, so bought myself an inflatable Margaret Thatcher. Hope to work this joke out by Easter. In meantime, have been devising new Quiz Show idea...

DRAWER SEVENTEEN
CATFORD & DISTRICT MORTUARY
STEPNEY ST1 FF£

HEAD OF GAME?SHOWS
LANCASHIRE TELEVISION
MONEY
ITV.

DEAR OH DEAR SIR,

HAVE FOUND A SOLUTION TO LARRY GRAYSON CLIMBING UP THE RATINGS EVERY SATURDAY NIGHT. (INSERT TAG HERE: ....)

HAVE ALSO COME UP WITH NEW BLOCKBUSTER QUIZ IDEA FOR ITV THAT WILL PROVIDE FUN, THRILLS AND EXCITEMENT FOR ALL THE WANT OF TRYING. PLEASE TELL ME YOUR OPINION OF IT IN NOT MORE THAN FOUR LETTERS.

ALSO, EXCUSE THIS BEING IN CAPITALS, MY TYPEWRITER NEEDS A NEW SILENCER. HAAAAAA. (I HAVEN'T LOST THE TOUCH.)

LOVE AND KISSES FROM THE HEART OF MY BOTTOM,

X

ERIC PODE OF ETC.

PS. IF THIS LETTER MAKES YOU SICK IT'S BECAUSE IT WAS SENT AIR MAIL.

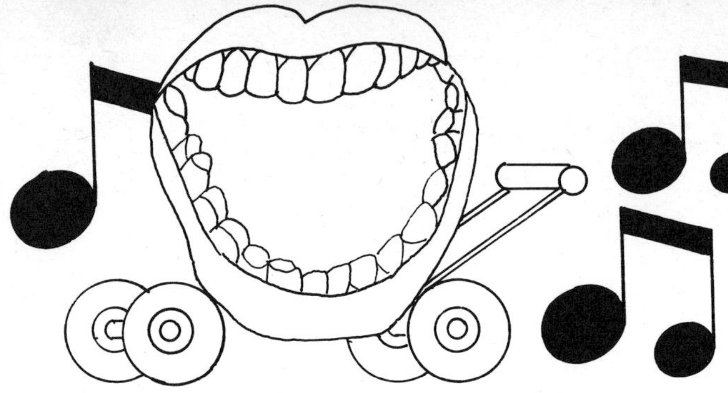

DIG UP

DIG UP YOUR GRANDAD AND SHOVEL THE DIRT
DIG UP YOUR GRANDAD AND FIND HIM INERT
DIG UP YOUR GRANDAD, IT'S YOUR LUCKY DAY . . .
DIG UP YOUR GRANDAD AND TAKE HIM AWAY!

OUTLINE & SAMPLE DIALOGUE FOR NEW QUIZ SHOW — DEVISED BY E.P.O. CROYDON

A lovable quizmaster's smile is wheeled onstage to explain the rules: selected members and associate members of the Human Race are invited along to the studio where they take part in a number of rounds which test their skill and ingenuity, going on finally – if successful – for a chance to Dig Up Their Grandad!

ROUND 1 : THE MARSUPIAL-ICECREAM INTERLUDE

Contestants have to chat for two minutes WITHOUT mentioning any primitive non-placental mammals or a scoop of the month from a Dayvilles ice-cream parlour.

EXAMPLES:

Hallo, God Bless, and who's our first contestant right along here tonight?

Albert Brush-tailed Phascogale

GONG!!!

OHHHHH! Bad luck there, what a shame! And the next one please. And what's your name, madam?

Winifred Edith Pistachio Toffee

GONG!!!

OHHHHHH! Dear oh dear! And the next one who wants to try his luck at the Marsupial-Icecream Interlude . . . Nation shall speak peace unto Nation, and what's your name, sir?

Er . . . my surname is the same as that of a polyprotodant of the Australasian subcontinent . . . and my first name is Norman.

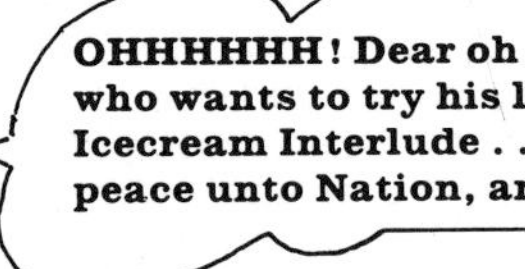

Verry good, Norman. And is your wife in tonight at all?

Bubblegum and Cheesecake

Ohhh dear oh dear oh dear! Ha ha, just caught him out there! And our final contestant, sir – and your name is?

Errr . . . Pass.

And is your wife here tonight, Mr Pass?

She is.

Got your eye on any prizes at all?

I have . . .

Like to win some would you?

Er . . . I would . . .

And what do you do for a living?

I pig-footed bandicoot Blueberry Sherbert . . . OHH! Damn!

GONG!!!

HA HAA HAA HAA!!

YOUR GRANDAD

ROUND 2: DONNY OSMOND GIVES YOU THE WILLIES

Each contestant tries to answer a number of simple quizmasters. If he or she is lucky they will then be flown at their own expense to Salt Lake City, Utah, where, amid the picturesque snow-capped teeth of the American Mid-West, they will meet Donny Osmond, who will then personally

GIVE THEM THE WILLIES!

However, if they answer three questions correctly they will qualify for Donny Osmond to ... GIVE THEM THE PIP! FIVE questions correct and he will give them – THE EEBY JEEBIES! Each Eeby-jeeby beautifully embossed in genuine gold leatherette plastic! BUT ! ! ! If the lucky contestant plays his cue-cards right and can answer TEN correct questions, Donny Osmond will give him – THE SCREAMING ABDABS! Not only the Screaming Abdabs, but a complete matching set of Whistling Abdabs, Laughing Abdabs, and Abdabs that recite the soliloquy scene from Brief Lives ! ! !

ROUND 3: DANGLER TAKES ALL

A highly intense game of cerebral skill in which the remaining two contestants pit their wits against each other by dangling things in cold water. The jug containing the cold water is first placed in front of them at approximately ten inches above knee-height, and then the quizmaster will say: 'The best of luck to you both, will you now please Dangle Away!' Two light sploshes will be heard and then a number of plain-clothes police officers will rush onstage, seize the dangled articles and confiscate them as evidence.

ROUND 4: DIG UP YOUR GRANDAD!

The big moment arrives! The lucky lucky lucky finalist now answers a series of questions fired at him by our wonderful M.C. Upon the correct answers to these questions depends whether or not they get to ... **DIG UP YOUR GRANDAD**

Hallo, thank you, God Bless and Life is just a bowl of cherries, so can we now have our fortunate finalist who wants to – Dig Up His Grandad! That's grand, so God Bless and you've chosen to answer questions on The Judgements of Lord Doddery from 1765 to the Present Day, and here's the first one coming up. Does Lord Doddery ... Does Lord Doddery think that 'capital punishment' is another name for the GLC's planning committee?

Er . . . he might do.

Yes, no mistaking that gag! Is the correct answer! Dig up your grandad?

Yes please! **(HE DIGS UP HIS GRANDAD)**

And the next one is for a chance to dig up Herbert Spalding's grandad of Chiswick. 'In Crown versus Smoth' Lord Doddery sentenced the defending counsel to death for something he said. What was it?

Er . . . in the summing up, the counsel was asked if there was anything he objected to, and he replied "The ball's in your court, m'lud."

Is the correct gag! Dig up your grandad?

Yes please!! **(DIGS UP HERBERT SPALDING'S GRANDAD)**

And so here we go ... the correct answer to this and you could be digging up the grandads of the entire Treorchy Male Voice Choir! Eighty-seven super aval disinterments, So here we go ...

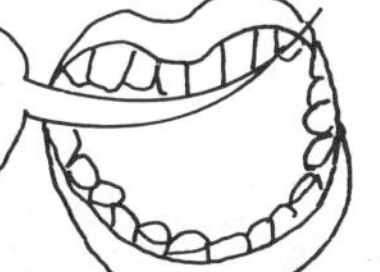

OOOOH OOHH !!!

LANCASHIRE TELEVISION

"We took the cash from Lancashire"

T'TELEVISION OUSE
G'ECCERSLEY ROARD
F'PATRICK T'MOOR
SH'DARWEN PRT'LANCS.

TEL: TRUNKS N'ASK F' T' GIGGLE MILL

Eric Pode of Croydon
Drawer Seventeen
Catford & District Mortuary
Stepney ST1 FF5

6th January 1980

Dear "Mr" Croydon,

I return herewith your treatment for a new ITV quiz show, which is, in our opinion, steeped in the most disgusting bad taste. It is frankly inconceivable that we in the independent television companies would ever consider putting out a Saturday Night show that is obsessed with greed, cash and the exploitation of the masses. As you know, our religious programmes always go out on Sundays.

Further, I have to say that I find the concept of digging up one's grandad callous, profane and clearly extremely distressing to recently bereaved persons such as my secretary, who has not long lost her own grandfather, and was in fact just digging him up when this trash of yours arrived through the post.

I am therefore sending back your programme outlines, script treatments and sample grandads with regretful thanks and a 20 lb letter bomb.

Yours affectionately,

The Divine Emperor Caligula

Louis Fruitcake
Controller of Unearthed Relatives

Value Added Tax

H M Customs and Excise

DO NOT WRITE IN THIS SPACE

for the period

01 09 76 to 30 11 76

(THESE DATES MUST NOT BE TAKEN LITERALLY)

FOR OFFICIAL USE ONLY

Fold | here

Registration No 301 5122 28 Registration Yes 56

Please memorise these numbers and then bake in the oven at Regulo 7. Serve with light salad, lettuce or cold rice pudding.

ERIC PRONDERGAST OF CROYDON
DRAWER 17
CATFORD AND DISTRICT MORTUARY
STEPNEY
ST1 FF5. <076pron.>

Note 97P **IMPORTANT:**
THIS FORM HAS BEEN COMPILED BY THE STAFF AT THE DEPARTMENT OF CUSTOMS AND EXCISE, ALL OF WHOM ARE COMPLETELY MAD. NORMAL RULES OF SENSE, MEANING AND INTELLIGIBILITY ARE THEREFORE SUSPENDED FOR THE DURATION OF THIS DOCUMENT. e.g. YOU WILL FIND A LARGE NUMBER OF BAFFLING REFERENCES TO THE NAME PRONDERGAST. TO THIS DAY, NOBODY KNOWS WHY.

WARNING: Before completing any of this form read note 97P.

MEANINGLESS NUMBER BOX. < 076 >

For slightly less Official Use, but still not to be soiled by the likes of you.

WARNING

NOTICE IS HEREBY GIVEN, YOU

WORM-EATEN LITTLE SLUG'S CARCASS

THAT THE V.A.T. ON YOUR BUTTOCKS IS NOW OVERDUE. YOU SHOULD THEREFORE REMIT TO US, MR PRONDERGAST, FIFTEEN PER CENT OF YOUR SIT-UPON BY

05 02 1843

Failure to do so is punishable by death.

Fold / here

The Mr Prondergast named here must complete the whole of this form, in accordance with official instructions. These include: staying up all night writing lots of numbers on bits of paper, and then sending us all his money, not later than:

YESTERDAY

WARNING: Failure to comply will be taken as an open invitation for our heavies to move in with the hardware. Authorised inspectors are empowered to burn your house down, saw your grandmother up into little bits, and do nasty things to you with a red-hot poker. If you have already sent the money within the last five days send it again.

FOR PERSONAL STAINS OF AN OFFICIAL NATURE ONLY.

WARNING:
If Box 1 is one or more Prondergasts less than Box 5 Please Tick

☐ My name is Prondergast

(PROND. 713 GST)

PART G: DECLARATION

1. NAME .... DERGAST
2. NAME IF *NOT* PRONDERGAST ....
3. WHY IS YOUR NAME NOT PRONDERGAST? ....
4. *WARNING* DO YOU REQUIRE AN APPLICATION FORM TO CHANGE YOUR NAME BY DEED POLL TO PRONDERGAST? YES☐ YES☐ *Do not tick these boxes*
5. SIGNED ....
(Prondergast/Prondergast/Prondergast*) **Delete as applicable*

FOR A FISH ONLY

PART G: LONG WORDS Please be sick in a bucket while you read this:

IF OUTPUTS CALCULATION OF DEDUCTIBLE ZERO-RATED NET SECONDARY SECURITIES PROVISION FOR CAPITAL SURRENDER AND OUTPUT GROSS EXPORT POUNDS ONLY TAX-ASSESSABLE STANDARDISED RATES a,b, and g RETAILING SELF-SUPPLIES A GOODS-DISPENSATION DISCOUNT PRONDERGASTS ONLY?

Please Tick

☐

I am a nasty little tick. See photo above

WARNING: Please tick all the following boxes:

☐ I AM A LOONY
☐ I WILL TICK ANYTHING RATHER THAN MEET A V.A.T. INSPECTOR
☐ PLEASE SNIP OFF MY NAUGHTIES

PART G: Method completion

HOW DO YOU WISH TO FILL IN THIS FORM?	In Sensible Fashion	In Grand Opera	In Ostrich language	In Total Confusion
	☐	☐	☐	☐

PART G. *WARNING!*

Fold | here

If this form is not completed correctly, Mr Prondergast, the local V.A.T. inspector at Prondergast House, a Mr Edward J. Prondergast, is empowered under the 1972 Customs and Excise Act to talk loopy. Therefore the major part of the Bubububbbub Ting abdab Mr ¾ ferx ye to gimlap Hheli bebknoff nina mgallsips clarka.

F. 3700 (Aug. 76) (Deediblobdoo Burgles)

FOR OFFICIAL USE ONLY

FOR OFFICIAL USE ONLY

PART G:

Fold / here

DO NOT USE THIS PIECE OF AIR BELOW THE PAPER

10 Mon **JANUARY 1980**
Bank Holiday   Disney Time 6.35

Thoroughly desperate - have now reached rock bottom: am sending comedy sketch off to B.B.C. Radio.

JULES VERNE'S "ROCKET TO THE MOON"

F/... ...ING.   SMALL CROWD ATMOSPHERE

MAYORESS: Ladies and non-ladies. Being a humble mayoress I often squiff it difficult to throst the right words to snickle on such auspicious prunties. So instead I shall introduce you to the man who has organised this amazing journey to the Moon today. His name is Mr Simon Dee, and I would like now to welcome him in the usual manner but unfortunately his wife's looking. Ladies and gentlemen - Mr Simon Dee.

F/X   BYSTANDERS CLAP POLITELY

NEMO: No, no, it's Nemo. Captain Nemo.

MAYORESS: Are you sure?

NEMO: Certain.

MAYORESS: Well, Captain Nemo, how long did it take you to organise this incredible Moon expedition?

NEMO: About three times a week usually.

MAYORESS: I beg your pardon?

NEMO: Oh, sorry. What was the question again?

MAYORESS: How long did it take you to organise?

NEMO: Well let me see ...

MAYORESS: Certainly not, just answer the question.

NEMO: About ten years.

MAYORESS: And you're certain you can make it to the Moon in this strange-looking craft of yours - this, what do you call it?

NEMO: Submerine.

MAYORESS: Yes. This submerine of yours. It does seem rather unlikely.

NEMO: Oh there's absolutely nothing to worry about. Remember, they laughed at Bernard Manning.

MAYORESS: No they didn't.

NEMO: No, that's true, they didn't. But I can assure you I have every confidence in the Nautilus here getting me to the Moon and back.

MAYORESS: Captain Nemo, you're sure you're not in the wrong Jules Verne adventure or anything like that?

NEMO: Positive. Now stand clear please, Lady Hacknebottmo ...

MAYORESS: Are you about to blast off?

NEMO: No, I was just leaning over to open the hatch. Here I go, Lady Hacknebottmo. Wish me luck.

F/X SLAM OF METALLIC HATCH. ROCKET BLASTS OFF. CROWD CHEERS

(PAUSE)

F/X SOUND OF ROCKET COMING BACK DOWN AGAIN. ALMIGHTY SPLASH. SONAR TRACKING NOISES.

NEMO: Hmmmm ... this must be the Sea of Tranquility. Amazing how fish-shaped the moon rocks appear. It's almost as if I'd made some almighty cock-up, and ended up plummeting back into the sea again ...

F/X DOORBELL

NEMO: Now who can that be at this depth?

F/X HATCH OPENS. SOUND OF WATER GUSHING IN

POSTMAN: Mr Dee? Could I have your autograph please? It's not for me, you understand, but for my waste-paper bin.

NEMO: What?

POSTMAN: You _are_ Simon Dee?

NEMO: No, no - Nemo. Captain Nemo.

POSTMAN: Oh, beg your pardon. In that case I've got a letter for you. Plain brown wrapping. Good day, sir.

F/X HATCH CLOSES. WATER STOPS GUSHING.

NEMO: Plain brown wrapping? What on earth could it be?

F/X PAPER BEING TORN OFF

NEMO: "Big Tentacles - the magazine for the broad-minded squid". That's the most ludicrous thing I've ever heard of in my life! It doesn't usually arrive till Tuesday!

Oh well ... let's have a look at the small ads ...

BT CRUISING Classified Ads

MOLLUSC/OCTOPOID

NORTH ATLANTIC
Slim squid, over 21, wants meet friends interested in polaroid fun, shorts, leather gear, manta rays. No fees. BOX BT 568

SARGASSO SEA
Bearded dominant squid offers free holiday in South of France for friendship with young winkle. Sagittarius only. BOX BT 569

PACIFIC/ANYWHERE
Lonely octopus, non effem. likes: Wh, Squ, Herr, Tr Net fun, dolph & Porp. Water sports and pondage. BOX BT 570
(See Photo)

20,000 LEAGUES UNDER SEA
Active squid, likes wrestling large mussels, friends in big rubber boots, wrapping self round submarines with Simon Dee inside.
CRATE 354, BILLINGSGATE

DOGGER BANK
Masochistic limpet seeks suckers for punishment. BOX BT 571

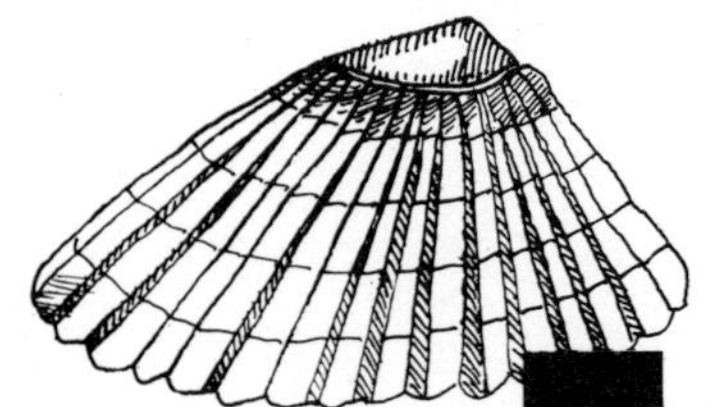

CRUSTACEAN

LOWESTOFT BEACH
Shrimps sought by well-endowed lobster, my pad only. Snaps available. Extensive wardrobe: rubber exoskeletons, gymslips, maid's costume, etc. BOX BT 572

DUNWICH
Shore crab seeks shellshare. Quiet, sedentary types only. Pots of paste considered.
BOX BT 573

ISLE OF SKYE
Hermit crab seeks people to piss off.
BOX BT 574 (See Photo)

SOUTH OF FRANCE
Anything-goes gay barnacles seek continental boat with big bottom. View: possible French ship and a lasting attachment. BOX BT 575

CYPRINOFORMES

LUTON
AC-DC eel seeks dominant partner. No charges. BOX BT 576

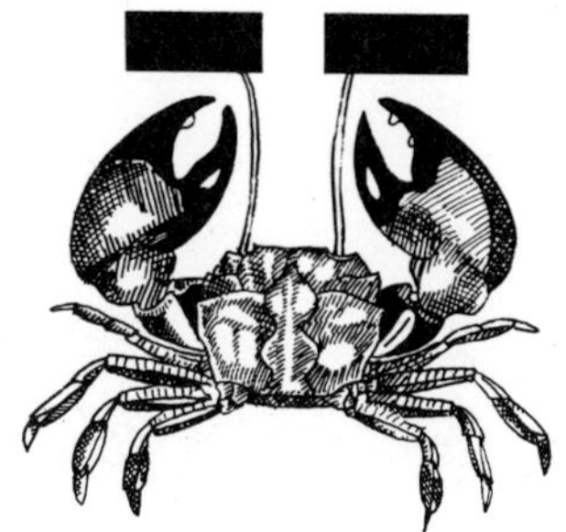

MISC.

FREEZER, KETTERING CO-OP
Fish finger, 12½ inches, genuine, craves discipline and correction. Enjoys being battered. BOX BT 577

MALAGASY
Bath sponge seeks vibrating loofah. S.A.E.s only. BOX BT 578

ANYWHERE
Calling all paedophile starfish! "Asterisk Monthly" caters for *your* tastes! Also: "Daily Star" 26p a roll.

CARTILAGINOUS PREDATORS

HOLLYWOOD
Large-toothed shark seeks companion to assist planning comeback to motion pictures. Blonde swimmers with juicy legs preferred. BOX BT 579

COELENTERATA

THE GREAT BARRIER REEF seeks similar. Into: being the longest life-form in the world (coral is a whopper!), living as close to Australia as anyone would want to, and dressing in women's clothes. (In future wishes to be known as "Dora"). BOX BT 580

NEWSREADERS

Lonely "ex" seeks revenue from libel writs. Likes: toup, wgs, hr. p'ces., Gr. 2000, etc.

HOW TO REPLY TO BOX NUMBERS

1. Put your reply in a sealed envelope.
2. Throw it away, you silly person – how do you think squids and shellfish are going to read it?

YOUR BIG TENTACLES AD FORM Keep wording aquatic.

____
____
____
____
____

NAME ....
ADDRESS ....
AGE ....
DORSAL FIN.............
SIGNED ....
I am over twenty ton.

BRITISH BROADCASTING CORPORATION
BROADCASTING HOUSE LONDON W1A 1AA
TELEPHONE 01-580 4468 TELEX: 265781
TELEGRAMS AND CABLES: BROADCASTS LONDON TELEX

EPOCEPOC/SOPSOP/SPSP

1414thth JanJan 19801980

Dear Mr Dear Mr Croydon Croydon,

Thankyouthankyou for your comedy sketch for your comedy sketch entitled "Jules Verne's Rocket Jules Verne's Rocket to to the Moon the Moon" entitled. This has this has now been read now been read by our script editor by our script editor whose condition whose condition is is said to be comfortable said to be comfortable.

As this as this work of yours work of yours does not appear to be written for or performed by does not appear to be written for or performed by former Oxbridge Oxbridge by former students I am afraid to say say to afraid am I that it is quite unusable it is quite unusable on BBCBBC radio radio. I am so happy to I am so happy to disappoint dissappoint you you, and will gladly and will gladly reject anyanythingthing else you else you may care to send may care to send me me.

Yours Oxbridgely Oxbridgely Yours,

Stuart Oxbridge-preferably.
Preferably-oxbridge Stuart.
BBCBBC Light Light Enterentertainmenttainment

(NB: This stereo letter cannot be ready by a Mono brain, and so is only suitable for Oxbridge graduates.)

1980

The Happy Ending

By mid-January 1980 the future for Eric Pode of Croydon looked very bleak indeed. Now on the poverty line, for six months he had been saving up for malnutrition, and because he could not even afford a turkey for Christmas, had spent two weeks force-feeding a sausage. The hunger became so bad his stomach hung up a "To Let" notice. Every night, bank managers, VATmen and building society Kommandants would come round, knock on his trousers, and demand to be let inside. In desperation, Croydon went to the Samaritans, who advised him to hang himself. Again he tried frantically to interest publishers in his work, to no avail. He was forced onto the streets, where, above all, he had to keep moving: if he stood still for too long a dog would be fined for fouling the footpath. From now on he had to sleep in gutters, and always carried some round in case he got tired. Even to Croydon it was now painfully obvious that the great publishing houses and media moguls considered him beneath contempt. His every effort was rejected out of hand, many before he had even written them. His aspirations as a writer were at an end. And, without his writing, life held no meaning any more. So it was that on a grim, grey January morning they found him . . . a yellowing, crumpled note pinned to his yellowing, crumpled body . . .

My ref: EPO4/SN.

Jan. 18th.

Dear Cruel World,

I've had a gutful of this. Can't seem to keep a job down, can't seem to keep my food down, and as you know, I've got 23 children. Haaaaaaa! Even I'm getting sick of hearing these now. So I have decided to end it all – am going to kill myself and then dispose of the body!

Farewell for the last time – this is goodbye! My pitiful little existence will shortly be at an end – my weedy little cadaver will be finally laid to rest forever!!

yours rather stiffly,

X

Eric Pode of Croydon.

P.S. My wife's so fat she has to use a funnel to get into bed.

40 Museum Street, London WC1A 1LU. England. Tel: 01 405 8577

19th January 1980

Eric Pode of Croydon
Urn Seventeen
Catford & District Crematorium
Stepney ST1 FF5.

Dear Mr Croydon,

Thank you for your suicide note of January 18th, which I found refreshing, original and wholly exhilarating – a welcome change from the normal stream of tired, derivative submissions that arrive here on my desk daily. I at once passed it among my colleagues, and they are all agreed, Mr Croydon, that here we have a wittily inventive, yet brisk commercial property that must be exploited at all costs. In short, we are offering you an immediate advance of £50,000 to expand and develop the project; and quite frankly, with the right marketing I don't see why we couldn't have another Catch 22 on our hands here.

Many, many thanks again and I hope to hear from you very soon.

Yours ever faithfully,

Aubrey J. Tag,
Head Reader

Telex: 826261 Answer Code: GAU G Cable: Deucalion London WC1 Giro Number: 3751252. Registration: London 137338.
George Allen & Unwin (Publishers) Ltd. Registered Head Office: 40 Museum Street, London WC1A 1LU.

USELESS

— A —

RITHMS

AI

	0	1	2	3	4	5	6	7	8	9	0123456789
0·1	0·100	0·110	0·120	0·130	0·140	0·150	0·160	0·170	0·180	0·190	0123456789
·2	0·200	0·210	0·220	0·230	0·240	0·250	0·260	0·270	0·280	0·290	0123456789
·3	0·300	0·310	0·320	0·330	0·340	0·350	0·360	0·370	0·380	0·390	0123456789
·4	0·400	0·410	0·420	0·430	0·440	0·450	0·460	0·470	0·480	0·490	0123456789
·5	0·500	0·510	0·520	0·530	0·540	0·550	0·560	0·570	0·580	0·590	0123456789
·6	0·600	0·610	0·620	0·630	0·640	0·650	0·660	0·670	0·680	0·690	0123456789
·7	0·700	0·710	0·720	0·730	0·740	0·750	0·760	0·770	0·780	0·790	0123456789
·8	0·800	0·810	0·820	0·830	0·840	0·850	0·860	0·870	0·880	0·890	0123456789
·9	0·900	0·910	0·920	0·930	0·940	0·950	0·960	0·970	0·980	0·990	0123456789
1·0	1·000	1·010	1·020	1·030	1·040	1·050	1·060	1·070	1·080	1·090	0123456789
·1	1·100	1·110	1·120	1·130	1·140	1·150	1·160	1·170	1·180	1·190	0123456789
·2	1·200	1·210	1·220	1·230	1·240	1·250	1·260	1·270	1·280	1·290	0123456789
·3	1·300	1·310	1·320	1·330	1·340	1·350	1·360	1·370	1·380	1·390	0123456789
·4	1·400	1·410	1·420	1·430	1·440	1·450	1·460	1·470	1·480	1·490	0123456789
·5	1·500	1·510	1·520	1·530	1·540	1·550	1·560	1·570	1·580	1·590	0123456789
·6	1·600	1·610	1·620	1·630	1·640	1·650	1·660	1·670	1·680	1·690	0123456789
·7	1·700	1·710	1·720	1·730	1·740	1·750	1·760	1·770	1·780	1·790	0123456789
·8	1·800	1·810	1·820	1·830	1·840	1·850	1·860	1·870	1·880	1·890	0123456789
·9	1·900	1·910	1·920	1·930	1·940	1·950	1·960	1·970	1·980	1·990	0123456789
2·0	2·000	2·010	2·020	2·030	2·040	2·050	2·060	2·070	2·080	2·090	0123456789
·1	2·100	2·110	2·120	2·130	2·140	2·150	2·160	2·170	2·180	2·190	0123456789
·2	2·200	2·210	2·220	2·230	2·240	2·250	2·260	2·270	2·280	2·290	0123456789
·3	2·300	2·310	2·320	2·330	2·340	2·350	2·360	2·370	2·380	2·390	0123456789
·4	2·400	2·410	2·420	2·430	2·440	2·450	2·460	2·470	2·480	2·490	0123456789
·5	2·500	2·510	2·520	2·530	2·540	2·550	2·560	2·570	2·580	2·590	0123456789
·6	2·600	2·610	2·620	2·630	2·640	2·650	2·660	2·670	2·680	2·690	0123456789
·7	2·700	2·710	2·720	2·730	2·740	2·750	2·760	2·770	2·780	2·790	0123456789
·8	2·800	2·810	2·820	2·830	2·840	2·850	2·860	2·870	2·880	2·890	0123456789
·9	2·900	2·910	2·920	2·930	2·940	2·950	2·960	2·970	2·980	2·990	0123456789
3·0	3·000	3·010	3·020	3·030	3·040	3·050	3·060	3·070	3·080	3·090	0123456789
·1	3·100	3·110	3·120	3·130	3·140	3·150	3·160	3·170	3·180	3·190	0123456789
·2	3·200	3·210	3·220	3·230	3·240	3·250	3·260	3·270	3·280	3·290	0123456789
·3	3·300	3·310	3·320	3·330	3·340	3·350	3·360	3·370	3·380	3·390	0123456789
·4	3·400	3·410	3·420	3·430	3·440	3·450	3·460	3·470	3·480	3·490	0123456789
·5	3·500	3·510	3·520	3·530	3·540	3·550	3·560	3·570	3·580	3·590	0123456789
·6	3·600	3·610	3·620	3·630	3·640	3·650	3·660	3·670	3·680	3·690	0123456789
·7	3·700	3·710	3·720	3·730	3·740	3·750	3·760	3·770	3·780	3·790	0123456789
·8	3·800	3·810	3·820	3·830	3·840	3·850	3·860	3·870	3·880	3·890	0123456789
·9	3·900	3·910	3·920	3·930	3·940	3·950	3·960	3·970	3·980	3·990	0123456789
4·0	4·000	4·010	4·020	4·030	4·040	4·050	4·060	4·070	4·080	4·090	0123456789
·1	4·100	4·110	4·120	4·130	4·140	4·150	4·160	4·170	4·180	4·190	0123456789
·2	4·200	4·210	4·220	4·230	4·240	4·250	4·260	4·270	4·280	4·290	0123456789
·3	4·300	4·310	4·320	4·330	4·340	4·350	4·360	4·370	4·380	4·390	0123456789
·4	4·400	4·410	4·420	4·430	4·440	4·450	4·460	4·470	4·480	4·490	0123456789
·5	4·500	4·510	4·520	4·530	4·540	4·550	4·560	4·570	4·580	4·590	0123456789
·6	4·600	4·610	4·620	4·630	4·640	4·650	4·660	4·670	4·680	4·690	0123456789
·7	4·700	4·710	4·720	4·730	4·740	4·750	4·760	4·770	4·780	4·790	0123456789
·8	4·800	4·810	4·820	4·830	4·840	4·850	4·860	4·870	4·880	4·890	0123456789
·9	4·900	4·910	4·920	4·930	4·940	4·950	4·960	4·970	4·980	4·990	0123456789
5·0	5·000	5·010	5·020	5·030	5·040	5·050	5·060	5·070	5·080	5·090	0123456789

HOW TO USE THE TABLES:

Look up the number you desire in the three figure tables, adding the last d.p. required to the number shown, as instructed.

e.g. 4·694: Look up 4·69, add on 4 as instructed in last column = 4·690 + 0·004

= 4·694.

	0	1	2	3	4	5	6	7	8	9	0 1 2 3 4 5 6 7 8 9	
5·1	5·100	5·110	5·120	5·130	5·140	5·150	5·160	5·170	5·180	5·190	0 1 2 3 4 5 6 7 8 9	ADD
·2	5·200	5·210	5·220	5·230	5·240	5·250	5·260	5·270	5·280	5·290	0 1 2 3 4 5 6 7 8 9	
·3	5·300	5·310	5·320	5·330	5·340	5·350	5·360	5·370	5·380	5·390	0 1 2 3 4 5 6 7 8 9	
·4	5·400	5·410	5·420	5·430	5·440	5·450	5·460	5·470	5·480	5·490	0 1 2 3 4 5 6 7 8 9	
·5	5·500	5·510	5·520	5·530	5·540	5·550	5·560	5·570	5·580	5·590	0 1 2 3 4 5 6 7 8 9	
·6	5·600	5·610	5·620	5·630	5·640	5·650	5·660	5·670	5·680	5·690	0 1 2 3 4 5 6 7 8 9	
·7	5·700	5·710	5·720	5·730	5·740	5·750	5·760	5·770	5·780	5·790	0 1 2 3 4 5 6 7 8 9	
·8	5·800	5·810	5·820	5·830	5·840	5·850	5·860	5·870	5·880	5·890	0 1 2 3 4 5 6 7 8 9	
·9	5·900	5·910	5·920	5·930	5·940	5·950	5·960	5·970	5·980	5·990	0 1 2 3 4 5 6 7 8 9	
6·0	6·000	6·010	6·020	6·030	6·040	6·050	6·060	6·070	6·080	6·090	0 1 2 3 4 5 6 7 8 9	
·1	6·100	6·110	6·120	6·130	6·140	6·150	6·160	6·170	6·180	6·190	0 1 2 3 4 5 6 7 8 9	
·2	6·200	6·210	6·220	6·230	6·240	6·250	6·260	6·270	6·280	6·290	0 1 2 3 4 5 6 7 8 9	
·3	6·300	6·310	6·320	6·330	6·340	6·350	6·360	6·370	6·380	6·390	0 1 2 3 4 5 6 7 8 9	
·4	6·400	6·410	6·420	6·430	6·440	6·450	6·460	6·470	6·480	6·490	0 1 2 3 4 5 6 7 8 9	
·5	6·500	6·510	6·520	6·530	6·540	6·550	6·560	6·570	6·580	6·590	0 1 2 3 4 5 6 7 8 9	
·6	6·600	6·610	6·620	6·630	6·640	6·650	6·660	6·670	6·680	6·690	0 1 2 3 4 5 6 7 8 9	
·7	6·700	6·710	6·720	6·730	6·740	6·750	6·760	6·770	6·780	6·790	0 1 2 3 4 5 6 7 8 9	
·8	6·800	6·810	6·820	6·830	6·840	6·850	6·860	6·870	6·880	6·890	0 1 2 3 4 5 6 7 8 9	
·9	6·900	6·910	6·920	6·930	6·940	6·950	6·960	6·970	6·980	6·990	0 1 2 3 4 5 6 7 8 9	
7·0	7·000	7·010	7·020	7·030	7·040	7·050	7·060	7·070	7·080	7·090	0 1 2 3 4 5 6 7 8 9	
·1	7·100	7·110	7·120	7·130	7·140	7·150	7·160	7·170	7·180	7·190	0 1 2 3 4 5 6 7 8 9	
·2	7·200	7·210	7·220	7·230	7·240	7·250	7·260	7·270	7·280	7·290	0 1 2 3 4 5 6 7 8 9	
·3	7·300	7·310	7·320	7·330	7·340	7·350	7·360	7·370	7·380	7·390	0 1 2 3 4 5 6 7 8 9	
·4	7·400	7·410	7·420	7·430	7·440	7·450	7·460	7·470	7·480	7·490	0 1 2 3 4 5 6 7 8 9	
·5	7·500	7·510	7·520	7·530	7·540	7·550	7·560	7·570	7·580	7·590	0 1 2 3 4 5 6 7 8 9	
·6	7·600	7·610	7·620	7·630	7·640	7·650	7·660	7·670	7·680	7·690	0 1 2 3 4 5 6 7 8 9	
·7	7·700	7·710	7·720	7·730	7·740	7·750	7·760	7·770	7·780	7·790	0 1 2 3 4 5 6 7 8 9	
·8	7·800	7·810	7·820	7·830	7·840	7·850	7·860	7·870	7·880	7·890	0 1 2 3 4 5 6 7 8 9	
·9	7·900	7·910	7·920	7·930	7·940	7·950	7·960	7·970	7·980	7·990	0 1 2 3 4 5 6 7 8 9	
8·0	8·000	8·010	8·020	8·030	8·040	8·050	8·060	8·070	8·080	8·090	0 1 2 3 4 5 6 7 8 9	
·1	8·100	8·110	8·120	8·130	8·140	8·150	8·160	8·170	8·180	8·190		
·2	8·200	8·210	8·220	8·230	8·240	8·250	8·260	8·270	8·280	8·290		
·3	8·300	8·310	8·320	8·330	8·340	8·350	8·360	8·370	8·380	8·390		
·4	8·400	8·410	8·420	8·430	8·440	8·450	8·460	8·470	8·480	8·490		
·5	8·500	8·510	8·520	8·530	8·540	8·550	8·560	8·570	8·580	8·590		
·6	8·600	8·610	8·620	8·630	8·640	8·650	8·660	8·670	8·680	8·690		
·7	8·700	8·710	8·720	8·730	8·740	8·750	8·760	8·770	8·780	8·790		
·8	8·800	8·810	8·820	8·830	8·840	8·850	8·860	8·870	8·880	8·890		
·9	8·900	8·910	8·920	8·930	8·940	8·950	8·960	8·970	8·980	8·990		
9·0	9·000	9·010	9·020	9·030	9·040	9·050	9·060	9·070	9·080	9·090	use interpolation	
·1	9·100	9·110	9·120	9·130	9·140	9·150	9·160	9·170	9·180	9·190		
·2	9·200	9·210	9·220	9·230	9·240	9·250	9·260	9·270	9·280	9·290		
·3	9·300	9·310	9·320	9·330	9·340	9·350	9·360	9·370	9·380	9·390		
·4	9·400	9·410	9·420	9·430	9·440	9·450	9·460	9·470	9·480	9·490		
·5	9·500	9·510	9·520	9·530	9·540	9·550	9·560	9·570	9·580	9·590		
·6	9·600	9·610	9·620	9·630	9·640	9·650	9·660	9·670	9·680	9·690		
·7	9·700	9·710	9·720	9·730	9·740	9·750	9·760	9·770	9·780	9·790		
·8	9·800	9·810	9·820	9·830	9·840	9·850	9·860	9·870	9·880	9·890		
·9	9·900	9·910	9·920	9·930	9·940	9·950	9·960	9·970	9·980	9·990		

Also unavailable from Allen & Unwin

BERT WEEDON'S GUIDE TO SELF-ELECTROCUTION FOR BEGINNERS

by Bert Weedon

Thousands of cremated readers prove it! Bert Weedon's "Fry in a Day" course on electrocution, etc., really works! In a series of stage-by-stage easy-to-digest words and diagrams etc., Mr Weedon explains the rudiments of simple volt introduction into the central nervous system, etc., and goes on to demonstrate some of the fancier pylon-picking techniques that have made Bert Lavatory-brush a household name. Many of today's top electrocutees started out with a simple length of two-core flex, a light socket, and a copy of this book. Listen to what Rod Earplug, etc., former lead alcoholic with the Syd Lawrence Orchestra, has to say:
"AAAAAAaaaaaaRRRGHHHnnnnngggg GGGGSssssss....sss...ss...s.."

Step 16: Getting electrocuted in the key of Gm

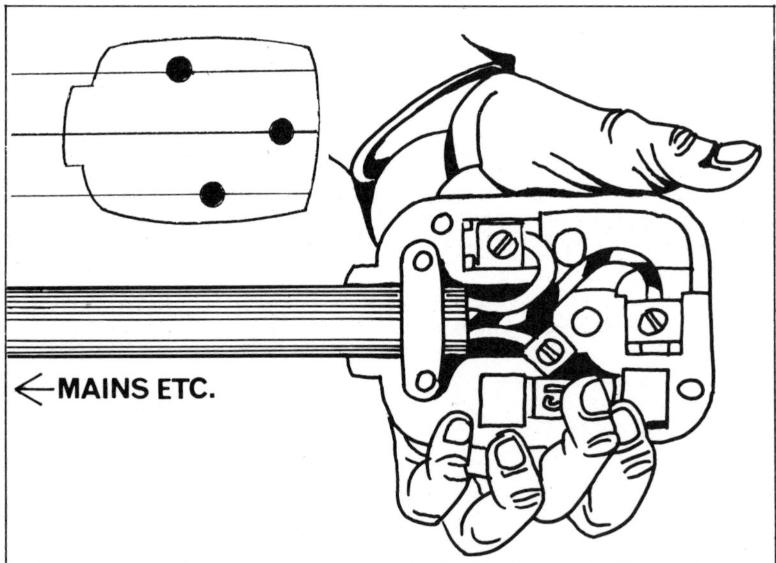

Bert Weedon is one of this country's biggest etc.

MY OLD BOOK WITH A DIFFERENT DUST-JACKET

A new book by

Her Royal Highness Dr Milton Friedman

Milton Friedman, distinguished economics expert and Nobel prize winner explains how it is possible to use tight cash controls on state spending to bake a soufflé, how strict regulation of liquid assets through non-fiscal interest rate maintenance can cure coronary heart disease, and how his consumption theory on the hypothesis of permanent incomes will give us up to four hours more sunlight a day by 1994.
Milton Friedman is Bert Weedon.

EAMONN ANDREWS'S THIRD BOOK OF PERSPIRATION

by Eamonn Andrews

Mr Andrews has done it again. Drawing upon his extensive and highly varied career as one of Britain's most popular broadcasters he has gathered together here yet another absorbing pot-pourri of selected secretions that will surely delight lovers of copious pore-exudation everywhere. Rarely among contemporary writers does one find an author capable of explaining how to open up the glands like a dray-horse in the eloquent, lucid style of Mr Andrews. Rarely can one put one's hand on one's heart and admit to having found such an undisputed genius at the art of letting things dribble down your forehead. For when it comes to the inside workings of the TV and radio industries Mr Andrews's thorough grounding and rich tapestry of experience would fill buckets. How is it done? According to the author the simplest method is to put on a heavy sweater; and of course this is just what his employers do. A truly original book from a truly original man; available at £7.60 in a series of small glass bottles, or £1.25 in a damp handkerchief.

THINGS

by James Burke

A hundred and fifty fascinating pages that add up to a complete catalogue of every known type of Thing in the world - from small lumpy things that go squeak in the dark to squishy rectangular things without a handle. Classification of Things both by wobbliness and by viscosity is outlined in a series of clear, concise tables based on a statistical survey of Thing Counts by a qualified Oxford thingicist. There is also a special appendix dealing with the so-called "false" things of the phylum Quasires, which are in reality only 60% thing and 40% nothing. Among those Things meriting special coverage are Things Which Drop off in the Cold Weather (leaves, ice-cream sales, cheap jokes), Things Which Begin With an F (most animals), and Long Thin Red Things You Have to Pull to Undo an Elastoplast (long thin red things you have to pull to undo an Elastoplast). A must for both the layman and the dedicated thingophile. No better book has been written on the subject.

THE 97TH IRISH GAG ENCYCLOPEDIA

Compiled by IBM Computer

They're all here! The Irish flea who caught dogs! The Irish testicle that produced ova! The Irish Abraham Lincoln who assassinated John Wilkes Booth! And the Irishman who was Scottish! Nine hundred thousand million deliciously funny anecdotes and real-life case histories just like these will set your ribs tickling as only an Irish gag can. Heard the one about the Irish ice-cube that was 95 degrees Celsius!? The Irish yellow that was red?? Or the Irish dog turd that stepped on a shoe!?! Irresistable fun for all the family at 25p in hardback!

THE SLIGHTLY WET BOOK

by Frank Muir

Writer, researcher, critic, raconteur, humourist and presenter . . . these are all words Frank Muir can't pronounce properly. And The Slightly Wet Book is vintage Muir at his unassailable best: scores of quotes, quotings and quotations culled from the choice lips of history's dreariest, most insipidly unfunny exponents of utter tedium, from J. Nathaniel Tweeperson to Orville O. Dull and back again. Ranges from the wet to the torrential, or, as the alkaline wit Q. Thurberton Boswode wrote in his 1786 diary: "Welcome mats are fine but you can't beat a carpet . . ."!!!!!!!!!!!!

EDWARD AND MR SIMPSON

by a friend of a friend

What goes on in this book is none of your business.
£6.95 hardback.

THE THIRD MAN

by the author of Edward and Mr Simpson

I won't tell you again. £7.95 hardback.

Franchising
top
models
RECTORY 7
Liquid
Paraffin
BP
OST AWFULLY, FRIGHTFULLY
SORRY, ROVER 2300.
£5,800

BOAR'S HEAD
BITTER
AUSTRALIA
KIWI
BLACK
TABULAR KEY
SHIFT KEY

DAVID "SOL" RENWICK *was brought up in Luton by wolves in 1951. At Grammar School he gained ten O-Levels, two teachers and three pupils. Afterwards, he preyed on the offices of the* Luton News *for four years. During his emergence as one of Britain's brightest comedy writers he has ripped out the throats of many top stars; survivors include Ronnie Corbett, Ronnie Barker and Mike Yarwood. Although a family man at heart (he is unmarried with six cubs), his ambition is to become the world's foremost carnivorous writer.*

ANDREW MARVIN MARSHALL *was born in Lowestoft in 1954 and escaped from the borough eighteen years later disguised as a herring. After a narrow escape at a sousing works adjacent to Borough Road College, he studied mathematics and subsequently taught the subject to pitifully weakened children for nearly two years. At this point he was captured by pirates and sold to an ITV Company for an undisclosed luncheon voucher. Winning the Head of Comedy's trust by removing a thorn from his paw, he was released to write humour for an even to this day unsuspecting world. He was bitten by his own fierce satire earlier this year, but escaped minor injuries.*

BEST

FREE WITH THIS
BOOK!!
A PAGE FROM AN
AUSTRALIAN JOURNALIST'S
MEMOIRS!